MISSISSIPPI

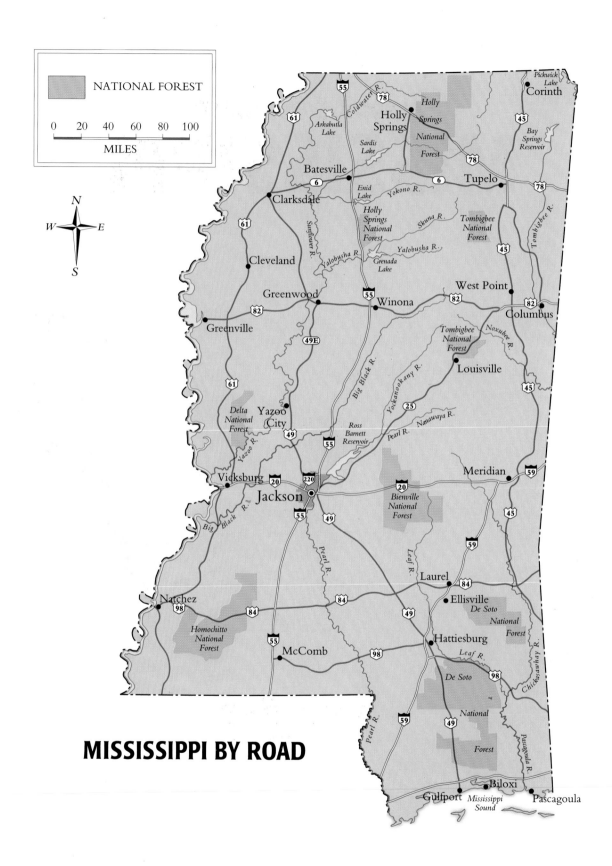

MISSISSIPPI BY ROAD

CELEBRATE THE STATES
MISSISSIPPI

David Shirley

BENCHMARK BOOKS

MARSHALL CAVENDISH
NEW YORK

To my mother and father

Benchmark Books
Marshall Cavendish Corporation
99 White Plains Road
Tarrytown, New York 10591-9001

Copyright © 1999 by Marshall Cavendish Corporation

Library of Congress Cataloging-in-Publication Data
Shirley, David, 1955–
Mississippi / David Shirley
p.   cm. — (Celebrate the states)
Includes bibliographical references (p.   ) and index.
Summary: Discusses the geographic features, history, government, people, achievements,
and attractions of the state whose name means "big river."
ISBN 0-7614-0664-6 (lib. bdg.)
1. Mississippi—Juvenile literature. [1. Mississippi.]
I. Title. II. Series.
F341.3.S55   1999   917.62—dc21   98-19496   CIP   AC

Maps and graphics supplied by Oxford Cartographers, Oxford, England

Photo research by Candlepants Incorporated

Cover photo: Stephen Kirkpatrick

The photographs in this book are used by permission and through the courtesy of: *Stephen Kirkpatrick*: 6-7, 10-11, 14, 19, 21, 22-23, 23(right), 26, 59, 62, 102, 117(top), 118, 123. *Image Bank*: Flip Chalfant, 13, 74, back cover; Eddie Hironaka, 46-47; Ira Block, 57; Walter Iooss, 70; Andrea Pistolesi, 106. *Peter Arnold, Inc.*: Clyde H. Smith, 16, 61, 69, 75, 76(bottom), 98-99, 111. *Photo Researchers, Inc.*: Tom & Pat Leeson, 17; Gary Retherford, 20; M. P. Kahl, 22(left); Geoff Bryant, 117(bottom); *Joslyn Art Museum, Omaha, Nebraska; Gift of Eron Art Foundation*: 28-29. *Peabody Museum-Harvard University Photo by Hillel Burber*: 31. *Corbis-Bettmann*: 33, 36, 37, 39, 40, 42, 43, 45, 126(right). *Robert Johnson-studio portrait Hooks Brothers, Memphis, 1935 ©Delta Haze Corporation, all rights reserved. Used by permission*: 85. *Archive Photos*: 91, 131; Ed Grazda, 88; Frank Driggs Collection, 92; Reuters/Sam Mircovich, 93; Frank Capri/Saga, 127; Lawrence Manning/Saga, 128. Scott Harrison, 129. Sara Krulwich/New York Times Co., 130; Ron Hershey, 133; *The Governors Office of Mississippi*: 50. *UPI/Corbis-Bettmann*: 53(top & bottom), 94, 96. *D. Donne Bryant Stock Photo*: D. Donne Bryant, 56, 72, 76(top), 77, 80, 82- 83; C. C. Lockwood, 120. *Omni-Photo Communications*: Jeff Greenberg, 66-67. *Ozark Yesteryear Photography*: Tom Coker, 107, 136. *Raymond Bial*: 101. *Mississippi Department of Economic and Community Development*: 113. *Nik Wheeler*: 125. *Reuters/Corbis-Bettmann*: 126(left). *Daily Mirror/Corbis-Bettmann*: 134.

Printed in Italy

3   5   6   4   2

CONTENTS

MISSISSIPPI IS . . .

Mississippi is a land of serenity . . .

"In the Delta, most of the world seemed sky. The land was perfectly flat and level, but shimmered like the wing of a lighted dragonfly. It seemed strummed, as though it were an instrument and something had touched it."   —Eudora Welty, novelist and short story writer

. . . and of suffering.

"The sun was too hot for too long, the rains too heavy, the soil too passionate for fruition, the vegetation too dense, the honeysuckle too sweet, the fields too flat. There was a doom on the land where I was born and raised."   —Writer David Cohn

Mississippi is the birthplace of the blues.

"The blues is an impulse to keep the painful details and episodes of a brutal experience alive in one's aching consciousness, to finger its jagged grain, and to transcend it."

—Ralph Ellison, novelist and essayist

"The blues ain't nothin' but a good man feelin' bad."

—Traditional blues lyric

It is a place to live . . .

"If we can ever find a way to solve our racial problems, Mississippi will be the best place in the world to live."

—James Meredith, the first black student
at the University of Mississippi

. . . to leave . . .

"That word—'Mississippi'—is perhaps the most loaded proper noun in American English. I would always be uneasy there, no matter what I did or how long I stayed. I knew too much, saw too many shadows and bad memories everywhere I turned."

—Writer Anthony Walton

. . . and to long for.

"Mississippi, you're on mind.
Mississippi, you're on mind.
Oh, Lord. Mississippi, you're on mind."

—Folk singer and former Mississippi resident Jesse Winchester, writing from his home in Canada

And it is still coming to grips with a troubled past.

"There's a lot of it I do want destroyed. There's a lot I want to keep."
—Newspaper publisher Hodding Carter, speaking about the Old South

---

Mississippi is a state rich in contradictions. It is a place known for its hospitality, as well as for its racial inequality. Plagued by poverty and illiteracy throughout its history, Mississippi has nevertheless produced some of our nation's most enduring music and literature. Perhaps more than any other state, it has been both a black society and a white society, with distinct barriers between the two. Today, the people of Mississippi are working together to resolve these contradictions and fulfill their state's promise.

1 A LAND OF GENTLE BEAUTY

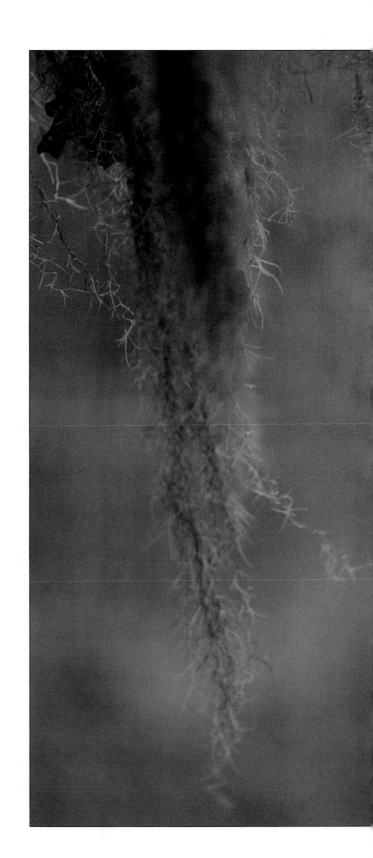

Mississippi is a small but beautiful state—two characteristics in which its residents take particular pride. "We're a modest little state, and we're proud about that," beams a farmer from Greenville. "You don't have to travel far to see things here, and there's plenty of beautiful things to see wherever you go. Unlike other places these days, we're not overrun with big cities and tall buildings and lots and lots of people. The beauty of Mississippi is still peaceful and undisturbed, and I really do hope we can keep it that way."

Mississippi ranks thirty-second in size among the fifty states. It stretches from the Gulf of Mexico in the south to Tennessee in the north. To the east, Mississippi is bordered by Alabama. The state's western border is defined by the smooth, muddy waters of the Mississippi River, with Arkansas across the river in the north and Louisiana in the south.

TWO NATURAL REGIONS

Mississippi is divided into two natural regions, both running north and south for the entire length of the state. In the west is the Mississippi Floodplain, while the East Gulf Coastal Plain occupies the rest of the state.

The floodplain covers the flat, narrow stretch of land that runs along the eastern bank of the Mississippi River. "The area around here is so flat," explains a truck driver from Cleveland, "that it feels sometimes like there's nothing but earth and sky. Things seem even flatter in the summer, when it's really hot and the sky gets hazy and heavy. Some days, these old narrow roads look like a long straight line that just stretches out forever."

For more than 15,000 years, the Mississippi River has frequently flooded, overflowing its banks and dumping rich black soil from upriver onto vast fields and marshes. The section of the floodplain between Yazoo City and the Tennessee border is known as the Mississippi Delta. The Delta is one of the nation's most important farming regions, producing huge crops of cotton and soybeans each year.

A small crop-dusting plane sweeps low across one of the flat, sprawling fields of the Mississippi Delta.

Wildflowers splash color along the shoulders of Mississippi's highways and back roads.

East of the floodplain is the East Gulf Coastal Plain. Unlike the flat, sprawling floodplain, the East Gulf Coastal Plain is covered with gentle, rolling hills. With much of the wooded land still undeveloped, the region is known for its tranquil, undisturbed beauty, its abundant wildlife and flowers, and its brilliant, star-filled night skies. "I love these forests in the early morning, before everybody leaves for work," says a construction worker from West Point. "There's no sound anywhere—even the crickets have stopped chirping—and the trees are so still and so silent that you can hear your own heart beat."

Mississippi's southern coastline is guarded from the Gulf of Mexico by a string of barrier islands a few miles offshore. The calm, shallow salt waters that form most of the state's southern border are known as the Mississippi Sound.

RIVERS AND LAKES

Mississippi is named after the majestic river that forms most of the state's western boundary. From its elevated shoreline in Natchez or Vicksburg, the Mississippi River is an astonishing sight, even to those who know it well. Its deep, muddy waters stretch out for more than a mile to the green Arkansas hills across the way, cutting and curving sharply as it stretches south toward the Gulf of Mexico.

The word *Mississippi* was coined by the Algonquin Indians and means "big river." In fact, the Mississippi is the largest river in North America. In the western part of the state, several major tributaries, including the Big Black River and the Yazoo River, empty into it. Across the rest of the state, a network of rivers and streams flow south toward the Mississippi Sound. The most important of these are the Pearl, Pascagoula, and Tombigbee Rivers.

Mississippi also has many lakes and reservoirs. The state's largest bodies of water, which were created by damming rivers, include Pickwick Lake, on the Tennessee River; Arkabutla Lake, on the Coldwater River; Grenada Lake, on the Yalobusha River; and Ross

In a familiar scene along the Mississippi, a team of tugboats push barges up the river.

Barnett Reservoir, on the Pearl River. Mississippi is also known for its oxbow lakes. These curved, narrow pockets form when flooding or high water upstream cause a river to change course, leaving the old path behind as a separate, self-enclosed body of water.

Throughout the flatter regions of the state—and in the gullies, ravines, and bottomlands of the hill country—the waters of creeks and streams sometimes overflow into wooded areas, forming swamps and marshes. Gum trees and cypress and tall oaks often rise out of these still, shallow waters.

A COLORFUL LANDSCAPE

Within Mississippi's borders, nature has painted an astonishing
variety of colors. From north to south, Mississippi's highways and
back roads are lined with endless rows of wildflowers. "Nothing is
more beautiful than our state's roadsides, especially in the spring"
says a merchant in Natchez. "Everywhere you look, you see the
magnificent colors of the wildflowers and the trees." Both rural

*In a moss-shaded swamp in southwestern Mississippi, alligators bask in the
noonday sun.*

areas and city streets are shaded by a variety of flowering trees and shrubs. The brilliant pink flowers of the azalea and the delicate white blossoms of the dogwood and magnolia are common sights.

Behind the whites, yellows, reds, and purples of Mississippi's flowers is the state's deep green landscape. More than 60 percent of Mississippi is covered with forests. The densely wooded hills of the north are made up of a variety of hardwood trees, such as hickory, elm, and blackjack oak. The area's many riverbeds and swamps are lined with cypress, live oak, sweet gum, and tupelo gum. Most of Mississippi's southern forests are filled with row after row of sharp-odored pine trees. "Every time that I leave the state," explains a truck driver in the small town of Wiggins, in the southeast corner of the state, "the first thing I notice when I get home is the strong, clean smell of those pines. You can say what you want, but the odor of pine trees is as much Mississippi as cotton or magnolias or catfish. It's the one thing that always tells me I'm home."

To the west, there are fewer trees and wildflowers, but the region's fertile soil is covered with the full green leaves and flowering blossoms of crops such as cotton and soybeans.

ANIMAL LIFE

Mississippi's forests and lakes are filled with wild animals. Until early in this century, cougars, wild boars, alligators, and bears were a widespread threat for the state's rural inhabitants. Today, smaller, less threatening animals roam the state's fields and forests, including opossums, foxes, rabbits, skunks, squirrels, and white-tailed deer, the state's most common large animal. With the

A morning fog settles over one of the dense pine forests of southern Mississippi.

abundance of wild animals and undeveloped land, hunting and fishing are popular pastimes for many Mississippians. The state's principal game birds are quail, duck, and wild turkey, and the most frequently caught freshwater fish include black bass, bream, perch, croaker, and catfish.

Mississippi is home to several endangered species, including the brown pelican, ivory-billed woodpecker, loggerhead turtle, and pallid sturgeon. The Mississippi sandhill crane, which is most com-

The opossum is common in the vast hardwood forests of central and northeastern Mississippi.

monly found in the marshes and swamps of the state's southern region, is also endangered.

One of Mississippi's endangered species is the red-cockaded woodpecker. The bird, which has a black body covered with tiny white specks, gets its name from the brilliant red stripe at each side of its black cap. Red-cockaded woodpeckers feed and nest exclusively in tall pine trees. The woodpeckers live together in small communities. They take turns guarding their nests and keep a steady stream of sap flowing from the holes that they bore around the nests. It's easy to spot the woodpeckers' nesting area by the huge sap stains on the tree trunks.

BYE, BYE, BLACKBIRD

In recent years, some of Mississippi's most serious ecological problems have actually involved the overpopulation of certain animals. As in many parts of the country, people are concerned about the steadily increasing number of white-tailed deer that crowd the forests and sometimes wander into residential neighborhoods. But the most troubling and spectacular problems have involved the state's bird population.

In the late 1980s, hundreds of thousands of blackbirds, cowbirds, and starlings began roosting each summer in a small patch of woods just outside of Tupelo, in the northeast part of the state. The birds' chirping was so loud that it could be heard inside the closed windows of cars speeding by on the Natchez Trace Parkway. And flying together, the birds occasionally darkened the noonday sky and actually prevented flights from landing at the local airport. After various failed efforts to frighten the birds away, park rangers and environmentalists were only able to disperse the birds by cutting down several acres of trees outside Tupelo. Mysteriously, the birds then abandoned the area, leaving the remainder of the region's dense forests undisturbed.

One of Mississippi's most endangered species, the majestic brown pelican, can still be glimpsed occasionally along the streams and tidewaters of the state's Gulf Coast.

Hunting and fishing are popular sports among Mississippians.

The endangered sandhill crane can be found in the marshes and swamps of southern Mississippi.

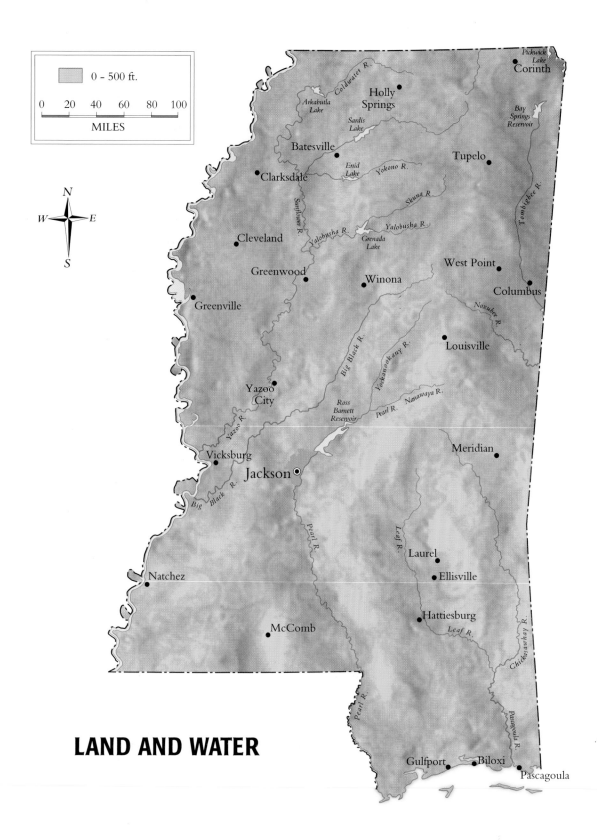

LAND AND WATER

The red-cockaded woodpecker has become threatened by the rapid harvesting of pine trees in Mississippi and throughout the Southeast. Many of the birds' nests have been accidentally destroyed by woodcutters, and large numbers of birds have been driven from the area or have died. There are now less than ten thousand red-cockaded woodpeckers remaining in the entire Southeast, many of them scattered throughout the pine forests of southwest Mississippi. Today, scientists, federal and state agencies, and the local lumber industry are trying to preserve the sections of forest where these rare birds live.

CLIMATE

"Mississippi means hot. That's all there is to it," explains a motel manager in Meridian. "From June to September, you can pretty much count on things here being hot and humid and miserable. And you'd just as well get used to it—because there's not a thing you can do about it."

Mississippi is known for long summers, short winters, and high humidity throughout the year. Mississippi winters are typically mild. Even the lightest snowfall is rare, and the average low temperature is well above freezing—hovering around 38 degrees Fahrenheit for most of the season. Summers are usually hot if not sweltering, especially in the southernmost part of the state. The thermometer frequently inches above the 100-degree mark during the long days of July and August.

Each summer all across the state, people do everything they can to fight the heat. Even the poorest, most rundown homes have air conditioners propped up on the windowsills. At outdoor occasions—like picnics, church socials, and sporting events—it is common to see entire crowds of people, especially older Mississippians, cooling themselves lazily with hand-held paper fans.

A high number of violent storms blow through the state each year. Mississippi ranks fifth nationwide in the number of tornadoes that touch down annually. These funnel-shaped whirlwinds often cause terrible destruction. When it comes to tornadoes classified as "strong" or "violent," Mississippi has been at the top

of the list for the past several years. Since the early part of the century, an average of fifteen people have been killed by tornadoes each year in the state.

In 1840, the most destructive tornado in U.S. history struck the city of Natchez in the southwest part of the state, killing 317 people. Almost one hundred years later, in 1936, another big twister demolished most of Tupelo, killing 216 people and seriously injuring 659 others. In August 1969, the Great Hurricane Camille smashed into the Gulf Coast. The storm caused heavy flooding and serious property damage for more than one hundred miles inland. Some people estimate that Camille's winds exceeded two hundred miles per hour!

But even after its worst storms, Mississippi becomes a place of gentle beauty once again. "There's nothing like right after a big storm sets in," says a store owner from Philadelphia. "Leaves and limbs are scattered everywhere. Things get tossed all which of way. But once it stops and the storm blows over, things get still and quiet. The air smells fresh and clear, and you see rainbows stretched across the road in front of you, sometime two or three at a time."

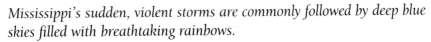

Mississippi's sudden, violent storms are commonly followed by deep blue skies filled with breathtaking rainbows.

2 A RICH AND TROUBLED PAST

View on the Mississippi *by Karl Bodmer*

At times Mississippi seems almost overwhelmed by its own history. All across the state, travelers encounter reminders of Mississippi's rich but troubled past. The great cotton plantations of the Delta recall the backbreaking servitude of the slaves and sharecroppers who cleared the land and harvested its crops. Parks and monuments throughout the state mark Civil War battle sites and memorialize the thousands of young men who died defending the Confederacy. Streets, high schools, and community centers in dozens of cities and towns proudly bear the names of slain civil rights leaders of the 1950s and 1960s. Even the state's musical legacy—the blues and gospel heard everywhere from barrooms to churches to concert halls—returns again and again to the injustice, violence, and finally, the dramatic changes that have swept across the state during the past 150 years.

FIRST INHABITANTS

Very little is known about Mississippi's earliest settlers. Hundreds of years ago, these people, known today as the Mound Builders, erected huge earthen pyramids at the center of their villages. No one knows exactly why the mounds were built, but historians believe that they may have served as foundations for important buildings used in religious rituals.

The Mound Builders were likely the ancestors of the Natchez Indians, who lived for centuries in southwest Mississippi on the land around these earthen mounds. The Natchez lived in small villages where they raised corn, beans, and squash. They also hunted, fished, and gathered wild berries and roots.

The Choctaw Indians also lived in southern Mississippi, while the Chickasaw lived farther north. Before the first white settlers arrived, the region's Native Americans frequently exchanged crops, tools, and clothing, and established a five-hundred-mile trade route between southwest Mississippi and central Tennessee. Years later,

The Natchez Indians, who lived in the southwestern corner of the state, were probably the descendants of the Mound Builders, the first people to live in the area.

this trail would be used by white settlers and come to be known as the Natchez Trace.

DE SOTO AND THE LOST CITY OF GOLD

The first Europeans to reach the area were led by the Spaniard Hernando de Soto, who landed in North America in 1539. After establishing himself as the colonial governor of Florida, he embarked on a quest to find the lost "City of Gold" that he had heard described in Indian legends. The following year, de Soto crossed into the area now known as Mississippi, near the current site of Columbus.

In Mississippi, de Soto encountered a large encampment of Chickasaws. At first, the Indians received the Spaniards peacefully. But when de Soto enslaved several of them and forced them to carry the supplies during the remainder of his journey, the Chickasaws fought back. One night, they attacked the Spanish campsite, setting fire to wagons and huts while de Soto and his men slept. When the smoke cleared, forty of de Soto's men were dead, and his livestock and supplies were almost completely destroyed.

With little except the clothes on their backs, the Spaniards fled the smoldering remains of their camp and headed west, where de Soto still believed he would find the City of Gold. A few weeks later, their march was halted by the vast waters of the Mississippi River. For de Soto, the awe-inspiring river was just one more obstacle in his quest for gold. He put his men to work building rafts, and they crossed the Mississippi into what is now Arkansas. In 1542, after months of wandering lost through the swamps and forests of

Arkansas, de Soto became ill and died suddenly. A year later, the few surviving explorers rafted down the great river into the Gulf of Mexico, never having found the lost City of Gold.

SMOKING PIPES OF PEACE

Another 140 years would pass before Europeans again ventured into present-day Mississippi. In 1682, the French explorer René-Robert Cavelier, Sieur de La Salle entered the region. La Salle was much more skilled at befriending the native population than de Soto had been. He was also more respectful of the importance of

The French explorer La Salle was the first European to make friends with the region's native inhabitants.

the great river to the west. He recognized that the Mississippi River was destined to serve as an important waterway in the New World, and he wasted no time in claiming its shores for France.

The powerful Natchez tribe had several large settlements along the river. La Salle visited their villages, smoking peace pipes and exchanging gifts with their leaders. For the next thirty years, the French enjoyed peaceful relations with the Natchez, and they expanded their claims to include outposts on the Gulf Coast.

Their luck quickly changed, however, in 1715, when territorial governor Antoine de La Mothe Cadillac offended the inhabitants of one Natchez settlement by refusing to share a peace pipe with their chief. The Indians expressed their anger by killing several of Cadillac's men, and many violent skirmishes followed between the French and the Natchez. In 1729, the French finally defeated the Natchez, driving them from their homes to lands west of the Mississippi River. The few Natchez who remained on the eastern side of the river eventually joined neighboring Chickasaw villages.

Toward the end of the seventeenth century, France and England began arguing over the ownership of their settlements throughout the New World. For the next seventy-five years, they fought a series of battles—known as the French and Indian Wars—over these disputed land claims. When the French finally surrendered in 1763, their settlements on the Gulf Coast and east of the Mississippi were claimed by the British. The British government returned Mississippi to its original Choctaw and Chickasaw inhabitants and declared it off-limits to all white settlers.

Even after the American colonists declared their independence and defeated the British in the Revolutionary War, the region that would become Mississippi remained sparsely occupied by white settlers for more than twenty years. Finally, with the formation of the Mississippi Territory in 1798, a few wagon trains of hunters, trappers, and farmers began setting up camps in the region.

Eventually, white settlers began pouring into the area, and the Chickasaw and Choctaw Indians were forced onto reservation lands in unsettled territories west of the Mississippi. By 1830, few remained in Mississippi.

SLAVES ARRIVE IN THE DELTA

By 1817, Mississippi had finally attracted enough settlers for Congress to name it the nation's twentieth state. At the time, very little of the state's land had actually been cleared for planting. When the first white settlers had arrived in the Delta, the land was an uncultivated jungle of forests and swamps.

But the Mississippi River and the rich soil spreading out from its eastern banks were too important for the young nation's economy to remain undeveloped for long. In the 1830s, wealthy developers from across the country began to purchase huge plots of land throughout the Delta. Their goal was to grow cotton on the region's dark, fertile soil. The invention of the cotton gin by Eli Whitney in 1793 had made it easier to remove the cotton seeds from the fiber. This turned cotton into one of the nation's most profitable crops.

Before the seeds could be planted and the cotton bolls could be harvested, however, the land had to be cleared of thickets and trees, and the region's vast swamps had to be drained. Between 1830 and

The invention of the cotton gin by Eli Whitney in 1793 turned cotton into one of the nation's most profitable crops.

1860, thousands of African men, women, and children were brought to the Delta as slaves to perform these grueling tasks.

In the 1500s, even before de Soto's expedition, the first Africans had arrived in what is now Mississippi as escaped slaves from Spanish colonies in the Caribbean. Most eventually became part of the Native American communities de Soto and his men encountered on the shore. When Mississippi entered the Union, slaves made up only a modest percentage of the state's overall population.

By 1850, however, three out of four residents of Natchez were African-American slaves. By 1860, slaves would outnumber white settlers by as many as six to one in the Delta's richest counties.

In just a few years, the slaves' hard, unpaid labor produced extraordinary wealth for their owners. Plantation owners used their newly acquired wealth to erect enormous homes, which they filled with expensive furniture and fine-art collections imported from Europe. In the old plantation system, the owners' great mansions usually stood side by side with the slaves' simple living quarters.

THE CIVIL WAR

The cultivation of cotton land in the Delta was brought to an abrupt halt by the outbreak of the Civil War on April 12, 1861. For several

The slaves who worked the cotton fields lived in tiny, wood-framed shacks a short walk from the master's large plantation home.

decades, Northern and Southern leaders had been quarreling over the relationship between the state and federal governments. Many Northerners argued for a strong central government, which would develop and enforce the same set of rules for all the states. Southerners favored a looser form of national government. Under their plan, each individual state would have much more authority in establishing the rules and regulations by which it was governed. In the years before the war, the issue of slavery became the central conflict between the nation's Northern and Southern leaders.

On January 9, three months before the war began, Mississippi had followed South Carolina to become the second state to formally secede from the Union. The rebellious states soon formed the Confederate States of America. To most white Mississippians, the state represented the very heart and soul of the Confederacy. The new nation's first president, Jefferson Davis, was a Mississippian.

From the early days of the conflict, Union commander Ulysses S. Grant knew that he must capture the city of Vicksburg on the Mississippi River to win the war. Vicksburg is perched on bluffs high above a sharp bend in the river. Confederate cannons lined the bluffs, easily preventing Union riverboats from transporting goods south to New Orleans. Grass-covered hills and ravines protected the city on all sides, making it virtually impossible to attack by land.

After months of assaults, Grant and his troops failed to capture the city. In March 1863, he decided to cut off the Confederates' supplies and starve them into surrender. The Confederate soldiers held out for almost two months—surviving largely on berries, mule meat, and sassafras tea—before they surrendered on July 4. After yet another two years of fighting the North claimed victory.

A colleague once called Jefferson Davis "a regular bull-dog when he formed an opinion, for he would never let go."

It took Union army commander Ulysses S. Grant and his troops almost two years to capture the port city of Vicksburg.

RECONSTRUCTION

Mississippi was in shambles when the war ended. Raids by Union soldiers had destroyed roads and railroad lines and burned many factories and farms. At the time the war began, only 10 percent of the Delta had been cleared for planting. Large planters were now left with huge tracts of land to be cleared but without slave labor to do the work.

The situation was hardly better for the freed slaves. Despite their new legal rights, African Americans often found themselves with no place to stay and no source of income. In the years that followed

In the years following the Civil War, thousands of black and white farm laborers in Mississippi became trapped in a new system of economic oppression, known as sharecropping.

the war, many freed slaves remained on their old plantations to work as hired hands for their former masters.

Over the next few decades, a system known as sharecropping became increasingly common in the Delta and throughout the South. Through this arrangement, laborers rented land, housing, seed, and supplies from landowners in exchange for half of the crops they raised. Workers hoped to eventually earn enough money to purchase the land outright, but this rarely happened. In fact, most sharecroppers sank deeper and deeper in debt to the landowners. In just a few years, the majority of black farmers in Mississippi were trapped in this new form of economic slavery—permanently bound to their employers by enormous debts.

In the years immediately following the war, the period known as Reconstruction, the presence of the occupying Union army insured that freed slaves enjoyed the rights and protections to which they were legally entitled. As the troops withdrew, however, the freedom of black Mississippians disappeared with them. Soon, blacks were prevented from voting and holding political office. By the end of the nineteenth century, a formal system of segregation, known as the Jim Crow laws, had been put in place. Blacks were excluded from many public places, including white schools and libraries. When black citizens were admitted to such places as theaters, ballparks, or public transportation, they were forced to sit or stand in special sections, usually in the back.

The Great Depression of the 1920s and 1930s was particularly hard on Mississippi. Early in the century, a tiny insect called the boll weevil had first appeared in the state's cotton fields. During the depression, the boll weevil invaded the cotton fields by the

Before the civil rights legislation of the 1960s, black Mississippians were often forced to use separate, segregated facilities.

millions. Entire crops were quickly destroyed, leaving both farm owners and field workers with no way to support themselves. Faced with poor work conditions—and often the prospect of no work at all—thousands of Mississippians left the state and headed north.

THE CIVIL RIGHTS MOVEMENT

The more than one million black Mississippians who remained in the state during the 1930s and 1940s continued to face violence

THE LEGEND OF CASEY JONES

Mississippi is known for its tall tales about the colorful characters who have lived and died there. One of the most colorful was the locomotive engineer Casey Jones. Casey liked to drive fast—very fast—along Mississippi's flat fields and marshes.

Jones was popular among the farmers and small-town folks who lived along his route. As he would roar past, they would wave to him from beside the tracks. At night, when they heard his trademark long, drawn-out whistle rise and then slowly die out, they would turn over in their beds and say, "There goes Casey Jones."

On April 30, 1900, Jones was driving a large, old train. As he and his assistant, Sim Webb, rounded a curve outside the tiny town of Vaughn, they saw an enormous freight train moving slowly along the side track a few hundred yards ahead. They knew they were going to crash. The two old wood-frame trains were far too wide to pass without smashing into one another. And with Casey gunning the old train at almost sixty miles per hour, he couldn't stop in time to avoid a collision. "Jump, Sim, and save yourself!" Jones yelled, as he threw on the brakes. Sim did jump, but Casey stayed with the train, pulling at the whistle to warn the workers up ahead. According to local legend, he still had one hand on the whistle and the other on the brake when his broken body was pulled from the wreckage.

and oppression. Things began to change dramatically, however, during the civil rights movement of the 1950s and 1960s. In 1955, a fourteen-year-old black boy named Emmett Till was dragged from his grandfather's cabin and murdered by white racists. A few days earlier, Till, who was visiting from Chicago, had made the fatal mistake of whistling at a white woman on the street. The black press in Chicago heard about the story, and it soon became headline news around the nation. Suddenly, the harsh, violent condition of race relations in Mississippi was being discussed and debated by people everywhere.

In the following years, thousands of Mississippians risked their lives and their livelihoods to bring racial equality to their state. They participated in protests, sit-ins, and voter registration drives. One of the key events in that struggle occurred in September 1962, when James Meredith became the first African-American student at the University of Mississippi, which was regarded by many people as the last stronghold of the white Mississippi ruling class.

A few months later, on June 12, 1963, Medgar Evers, a prominent civil rights activist, was shot in the back in his own driveway by Byron de la Beckwith, a member of the white Citizens Council. Beckwith, who had bragged openly about killing Evers, was acquitted of the crime in two separate trials. But the international news coverage surrounding the Evers assassination increased the pressure for the passage of the Civil Rights Act of 1964, which banned segregation in Mississippi and throughout the nation.

In 1994, Beckwith was tried a third time for his role in Evers's slaying. This time, he was found guilty and sentenced to spend the rest of his life in prison. Each day during the trial, newspaper

In June 1963, thousands of grieving supporters marched through the streets of Jackson to mourn the assassination of civil rights leader Medgar Evers.

headlines served as a painful reminder for adult Mississippians of one of the low moments in their state's history, and young Mississippians received a disturbing lesson about their past.

As painful as the experience was, the trial was also an act of healing for many Mississippians, as blacks and whites came together to acknowledge a past injustice. "People want to act like bad things didn't happen, and I understand that. But you can't get past something till you admit it happened," explained an African-American restaurant owner in Clarksdale. "That trial was something we needed. Something all of us needed—not just black folks—to let us get on with our lives."

3 MAKING AND BREAKING LAWS

The state capitol in Jackson

Each state has its own form of government and its own style of making, enforcing, and changing the laws by which it is governed. Throughout much of its history, Mississippi has balanced a conservative, slow-moving form of government with a radical, often violent, tradition of protest and social dissent.

INSIDE GOVERNMENT

Mississippi's government is divided into three branches: executive, legislative, and judicial.

Executive. Mississippi's chief executive is the governor, who is elected for a four-year term. The governor is responsible for preparing the state budget and developing policies in areas such as education, law enforcement, and economic development. The governor also decides whether to sign or veto (reject) bills that the state legislature has approved.

Mississippi has traditionally had one of the weakest executive branches in the United States. This is partly because up until 1988, the governor was forbidden by law to serve consecutive terms.

Legislative. The Mississippi legislature is divided into a senate with 52 members and a house of representatives with 122 members. All state legislators are elected to four-year terms. The Mississippi

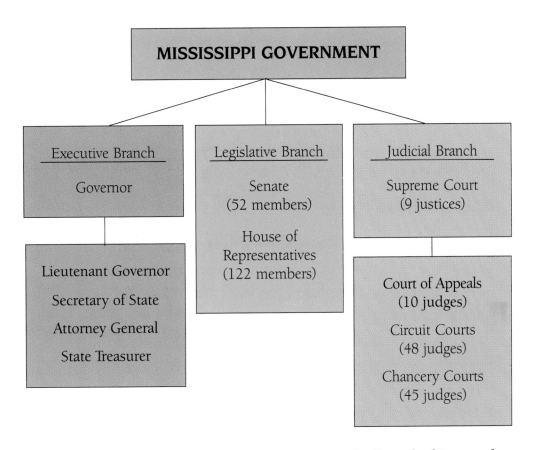

MISSISSIPPI GOVERNMENT

Executive Branch

Governor

Lieutenant Governor

Secretary of State

Attorney General

State Treasurer

Legislative Branch

Senate
(52 members)

House of
Representatives
(122 members)

Judicial Branch

Supreme Court
(9 justices)

Court of Appeals
(10 judges)

Circuit Courts
(48 judges)

Chancery Courts
(45 judges)

state legislature has enormous powers, including drafting and passing laws and public policy, approving budgets, raising state revenues, and overseeing the state's administrative network. If enough legislators agree, the legislature can also overturn the governor's veto of a bill, so it becomes law anyway.

Judicial. The state's highest court, the supreme court, consists of nine judges, who are elected to eight-year terms. The state's next highest court is the court of appeals, consisting of ten judges who are elected to four-year terms. Mississippi has two types of trial courts: circuit courts, which hear both civil and criminal cases, and chancery courts, which try only civil cases.

When someone challenges a decision in one of the state's criminal courts, the case is heard by the court of appeals, which decides whether to uphold or overturn the lower court's decision. If the court of appeals' decision is also challenged, the matter is sent to the state supreme court for a hearing.

POLITICAL PARTIES

Mississippi has shifted in the past thirty years from one of the nation's most Democratic states to a powerful Republican stronghold. From Reconstruction to the mid–twentieth century, Mississippi was commonly regarded as the center of the Solid South of the Democratic Party. Between 1876 and 1944, Mississippians voted for the Democratic candidate in every major local, state, and national election.

Following World War II, the legal rights of African Americans

Governor Kirk Fordice was the state's first Republican governor in more than a century.

became an increasingly important issue in national politics. In larger and larger numbers, white voters in Mississippi began to turn their backs on liberal Democratic candidates who openly favored desegregation and racial equality. After passage of the Voting Rights Act of 1965, more and more African Americans registered to vote, usually as members of the Democratic Party. But since the mid-1970s, Mississippi has become more Republican. In 1992, Kirk Fordice became the first Republican governor of the state since 1876. In 1978, Thad Cochran was elected as the state's first Republican senator since Reconstruction. He was joined in the U.S. Senate in 1989 by fellow Republican Trent Lott.

A DISSENTING PEOPLE

From the secretive activities of the racist Ku Klux Klan to the defiant public demonstrations of civil rights activists during the 1950s and 1960s, Mississippians have a long history of taking the law into their own hands. In fact, one of the few things that black and white Mississippians have always had in common is their open contempt for—and refusal to obey—laws they consider unfair or unjust.

In 1954, the U.S. Supreme Court declared the racial segregation of public schools to be unconstitutional. Calling this ruling "an illegal, immoral and sinful doctrine," Senator James O. "Big Jim" Eastland advised his fellow Mississippians not to obey it. "Southern people will not be violating the Constitution or the law," reasoned the senator, "when they defy this monstrous decision."

Almost a decade later, state leaders were still openly defiant of the Supreme Court's ruling and the power of the federal government to enforce it. In 1962, Governor Ross Barnett attracted international attention over his dispute with U.S. attorney general Robert F. Kennedy conserning the admission of James Meredith as a student at the University of Mississippi. "A segregated Mississippi, now and forever," Barnett proclaimed to a stadium full of defiant white Mississippians, just hours before giving in to the attorney general's demands.

Historically, black civil rights activists in the state have been even more defiant than their white, conservative counterparts in challenging laws with which they disagreed. During the 1950s and 1960s, hundreds of black Mississippians were thrown into jail for taking part in unauthorized demonstrations, or for refusing to obey laws that segregated citizens according to their race.

One of the bravest and most persistent of these people was Fannie Lou Hamer. Hamer spent much of the 1960s organizing protests, encouraging black citizens to vote, and teaching them to read and write. She was harassed and arrested for her efforts, once enduring a brutal beating at the Montgomery County Jail in Winona.

In 1964, Hamer took her fight for freedom to the Democratic National Convention, introducing the nation to the proud belligerence of Mississippi activism. Angered that the state's Democratic Party had failed to include African Americans in its delegation, Hamer led her own group of delegates into the convention hall. Officials refused to recognize Hamer's "Freedom Democratic Party" representatives. But she and her fellow delegates refused to leave, even when they were threatened with arrest.

The Democratic National Committee offered Hamer two tem-

The admission of James Meredith to the University of Mississippi in 1962 marked the beginning of the end for the state's long-standing policy of racial segregation.

In January 1965, Fannie Lou Hamer (center) and two other members of the Mississippi Freedom Democratic Party traveled to Washington, D.C., to request seats in the House of Representatives.

porary seats and promised full representation for black Mississippi Democrats in the future, but she rejected the compromise. "We didn't come all this way for no two seats when all of us is tired," she explained in a televised interview heard around the world.

Though Hamer's group was never seated, she did force convention officials to admit that the old policy for selecting state delegates was unfair. By the end of the convention, people everywhere knew a lot more about the racial inequities of both Mississippi politics and the national Democratic Party. And since then, black Mississippi Democrats have always been fairly represented at conventions.

EDUCATION

Illiteracy and poor education have traditionally been enormous problems for Mississippi. Today, roughly three-fourths of the state's adults are high school graduates, the lowest percentage in the nation. About 15 percent of all adults—both black and white—have less than a ninth-grade education. With limited classroom resources and salaries about $10,000 below the national average, teachers in the state face an uphill battle. "Sometimes I just want to scream," says a fifth-grade teacher from the Gulf Coast. "It's so hard to get these kids to realize the importance of a good education, when the adults around them do so little to support our schools—and our teachers! But these kids are what teaching is all

opposite: EARNING A LIVING

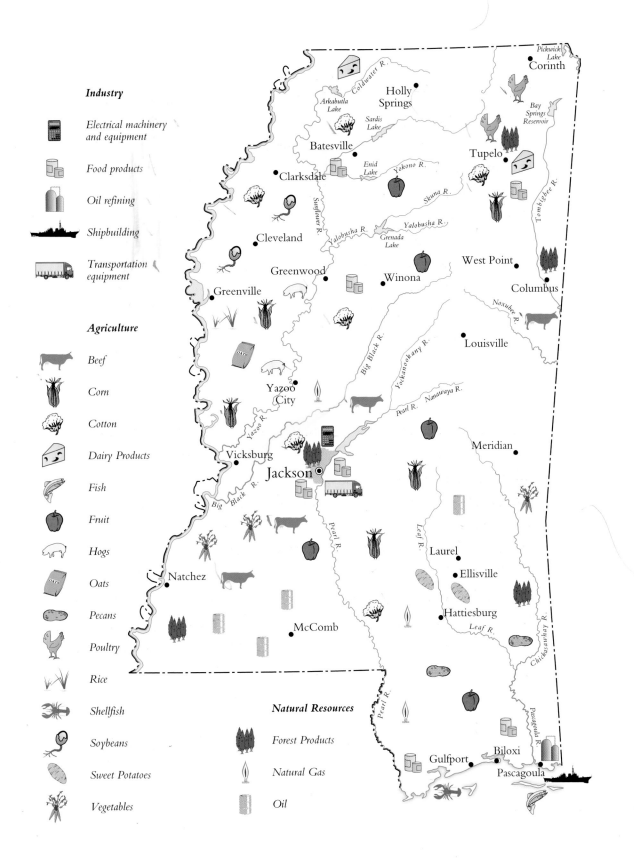

Industry

Electrical machinery and equipment

Food products

Oil refining

Shipbuilding

Transportation equipment

Agriculture

Beef

Corn

Cotton

Dairy Products

Fish

Fruit

Hogs

Oats

Pecans

Poultry

Rice

Shellfish

Soybeans

Sweet Potatoes

Vegetables

Natural Resources

Forest Products

Natural Gas

Oil

Pickwick
Lake

Corinth

Coldwater R.

Holly
Springs

Arkabutla
Lake

Sardis
Lake

Bay
Springs
Reservoir

Batesville

Enid
Lake

Yokono R.

Tupelo

Clarksdale

Skuna R.

Sunflower R.

Yalobusha R.

Yalobusha R.

Cleveland

Grenada
Lake

West Point

Greenwood

Winona

Columbus

Greenville

Noxubee R.

Big Black R.

Yakanookany R.

Louisville

Yazoo
City

Yazoo R.

Pearl R.

Nanawaya R.

Meridian

Vicksburg

Jackson

Big Black R.

Pearl R.

Leaf R.

Laurel

Natchez

Ellisville

Hattiesburg

Leaf R.

Chickasawhay R.

McComb

Pearl R.

Pascagoula R.

Gulfport

Biloxi

Pascagoula

The University of Southern Mississippi in Hattiesburg is the home of the prestigious literary journal The Mississippi Review.

about, and somehow, by stops and starts, they're managing to learn. And learning is so important for the future of our state."

In spite of its problems with education, Mississippi has an impressive set of colleges. Mississippi College, the state's oldest institution of higher learning, was founded in Clinton in 1826. The state boasts three major state universities. The University of Mississippi, in Oxford, is the home of the Center for the Study of Southern Culture, one of the leading folk history archives in the country. Mississippi State University, in Starkville, has one of the premier agricultural research facilities in the Southeast. The University of Southern Mississippi, in Hattiesburg, is the state's youngest major university and the publisher of *The Mississippi Review*, which has featured works by some of America's most gifted contemporary writers.

Cotton no longer dominates Mississippi's economy as it did during the first hundred years of statehood, but it is still an important cash crop.

ECONOMY

Most people find it hard to think about Mississippi without thinking of cotton. For its first hundred years of statehood, Mississippi's economy was devoted overwhelmingly to the production of cotton. A majority of the state's citizens made their living either as cotton farmers or field workers, or in some other part of the textile industry.

All this began to change in the 1930s, when the boll weevil destroyed thousands of acres of unharvested cotton around the state. It suddenly became clear to many farmers that it was too risky to base the state's entire economy on a single crop. During the next few years, large tracts of cotton fields throughout Mississippi were planted with peas, soybeans, corn, and grains. At the same time, the Balance Agriculture with Industry program was introduced to encourage the development of new businesses and the creation of new jobs in the state.

As a result of these changes, Mississippi farming is no longer the powerful economic force that it used to be. Today, profits from farming provide only 3 percent of the state's gross annual product. Livestock and livestock products make up more than half of Mississippi's farm economy, with crops (chiefly cotton and soybeans) accounting for most of the rest. Even with the dramatic reduction in cotton farming in the state, Mississippi still ranks as the nation's third-largest cotton producer.

If the large cotton plantations of the Delta no longer dominate

Today cattle and other livestock account for more than half of Mississippi's farm economy.

HUSH PUPPIES

Hush puppies, one of Mississippi's most popular foods, are usually served as a side dish with catfish or other fried foods. During the Civil War, Confederate cooks invented these deep-fried balls of cornmeal as a meager main dish for starving soldiers. According to one story, the dish earned its name because military dogs, which were often even hungrier than their masters, would scamper to where the hush puppies were being prepared and yelp loudly until they were fed. "Hush, puppies!" the cooks supposedly yelled as they tossed the dogs hot morsels from the pan.

Have an adult help you prepare your own delicious, steaming hot hush puppies:

Vegetable oil
1 cup white cornmeal
⅓ cup sugar
1 teaspoon salt
2 teaspoons baking powder
1 to 2 tablespoons minced onion
2 cups water
6 tablespoons butter

Using a deep skillet, heat 2 inches of oil for 60 seconds. Combine cornmeal, sugar, salt, baking powder, and onion in a medium-sized bowl. Combine water and butter in a small saucepan and bring to a boil over high heat. Pour over dry ingredients and stir rapidly to blend. When the mixture is cool enough to handle, form into 20 to 30 balls. Drop balls into hot oil a few at a time. Be careful not to crowd the pan. Deep-fry for 3 to 4 minutes, turning as often as needed, until they are golden brown on both sides. Remove hush puppies from oil and drain on paper towels. Hush puppies are best when served hot and in large quantities.

the state's economy, farming and farm life are still an important part of the state's appearance and personality. More than 40,000 active farms dot the highways and back roads of the state. The majority of these are small—350 acres or less.

The most significant development in the state's farm economy in recent years has been the introduction of catfish farming. In the Delta, hundreds of abandoned plantation fields have been converted into fish hatcheries. Today, Mississippi is the nation's leading

In recent years, Mississippi has become the nation's leading producer of commercial catfish.

producer of commercial catfish, with thousands of the fish shipped each day to restaurants and supermarkets around the country.

During the past two decades, industry has become a bigger and bigger part of Mississippi's economy. Today, manufacturing provides more than one-quarter of the state's annual income. One of Mississippi's largest industries is shipbuilding. A number of shipyards line the Gulf Coast, including Ingalls Shipbuilding in Pascagoula, the state's largest private employer.

Another growth industry is forestry and wood products. With more than half of its land covered by forests, Mississippi has tradi-

Forestry and wood production are one of the state's fast-growing industries. Here, logs recently harvested in southern Mississippi are shipped upriver to furniture factories in the northern part of the state.

GROSS STATE PRODUCT: $67.2 BILLION

(2000 estimated)

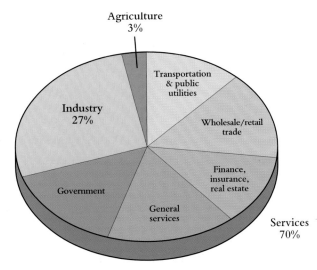

Agriculture
3%

Transportation
& public
utilities

Industry
27%

Wholesale/retail
trade

Finance,
insurance,
real estate

Government

General
services

Services
70%

tionally been a leader in harvesting pine and hardwoods. Today, the state ranks tenth nationwide in forestry production. Overstuffed logging trucks have long been a familiar sight on freeways across the state, and many small towns in the pinelands of the state's southeast corner rely heavily on paper mills for employment.

In the past, most Mississippi lumber was shipped out of state for manufacturing. This has changed in recent years, however, with wood-product factories opening up in such cities as Jackson, Columbus, and Natchez. Tupelo, in the state's northeast corner, has become one of the nation's major producers of hardwood furniture.

Tourism is also becoming an increasingly important industry in Mississippi. In the past few years, more than a dozen large gambling casinos have opened along the Mississippi River and Gulf Coast, making the area a major center for tourism and earning it the nickname the Playground of the South.

Despite Mississippi's many conflicts and hardships over the years, its citizens remain proud and determined. Today, both

POPULATION GROWTH: 1830–2000

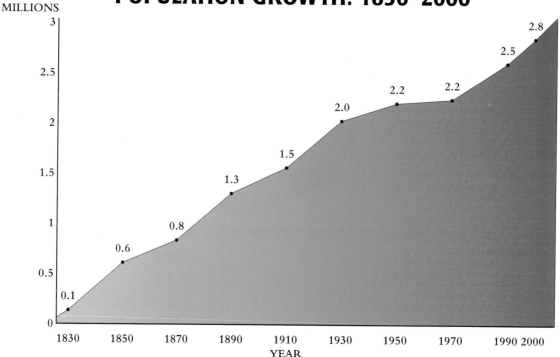

MILLIONS

3

2.5

2

1.5

1

0.5

0

0.1   0.6   0.8   1.3   1.5   2.0   2.2   2.2   2.5   2.8

1830   1850   1870   1890   1910   1930   1950   1970   1990 2000

YEAR

black and white Mississippians speak enthusiastically about the political and economic developments in their state during the past few years. And increasingly, members of both groups share a commitment to continue rethinking and rebuilding their state. "You have to admit," insists a teacher in McComb, "we have come a long, long way together. While the rest of the country was talking about the really tough issues—like desegregation and restructuring the economy—we were down here meeting them face to face. A lot of it may have been forced on us at the time, and some

A NEW BEGINNING

One of the most dramatic improvements in Mississippi's economy in recent years has involved the state's Choctaw Indian population. Virtually all of the more than eight thousand Native Americans now residing in Mississippi belong to the Choctaw tribe. Most of them live on a single reservation in the east-central part of the state. In the 1970s, the Choctaws faced widespread unemployment; less than one in four adults was able to find a job, either on or off the reservation. In 1979, the tribal council began planning the development of an eighty-acre industrial park, which they hoped would reverse the chronic poverty and unemployment among their people. In the past twenty years, the Choctaw government has developed many new businesses throughout the park, including a shopping center, automotive and electronic services, a variety of construction and manufacturing facilities, and an enormous resort casino. This has created almost five thousand new jobs, and more than 85 percent of the adult Choctaw population now have full-time employment.

of us may have come through it kicking and scratching, but we came through it just the same, and we're better people for it now. I think pretty much everyone realizes that."

4 COMMON GROUND

Since the earliest days of statehood, Mississippi has been divided along racial lines—a distinction that continues to separate many of the state's people. Beneath their deep-seated racial divisions, however, black and white Mississippians are surprisingly united about a number of other issues. The most important of these are their emphasis on friendliness and hospitality, and their common religious beliefs.

THE HOSPITALITY STATE

All across Mississippi, people take great pride in their state's reputation for friendliness and good manners. Mississippi has long been known as the Hospitality State, and Mississippians go out of their way to live up to the name.

From a tiny soul food café in the heart of the Delta to the sleek, fashionable shops of Jackson's Highland Village, visitors are always welcomed with the same friendly greeting. "How are *you*?" says the speaker, her voice rising and stretching the last word into two long syllables. "Just *how* can I be of help to you?"

"It's just the way we are, I guess, the way we're taught to be," explained a sales clerk in Gulfport. "I was always taught to say, 'Yes, sir,' and 'Yes, ma'am,' and to ask after people, even people I didn't know very well. Whenever I see somebody—either here at the store

Mississippians are great talkers. A simple request for directions is often answered with a lengthy conversation or a colorful tale.

or the rest of the time—I just naturally want to know who they are and how they're doing. And I think that's the way most people are in Mississippi."

In fact, one of the first things many visitors to the state notice is that it is virtually impossible to go anywhere—or do anything—without somehow ending up in a conversation. Complete strangers can be seen chatting together in bookstores and coffee shops as if they were the oldest of friends. Even the simplest questions are often greeted with lengthy, drawn-out replies. Ask someone on a

THE ANGER BENEATH
THE SURFACE

In the following passage from his autobiographical novel, *Black Boy*, Richard Wright describes how black Mississippians have frequently been forced to hide their ambitions and frustrations behind a protective veil of civility and good manners.

I began to marvel at how smoothly the black boys acted out the roles that the white race had mapped out for them. Most of them were not conscious of living a special, separate, stunted way of life. Yet I knew that in some period of their growing up—a period that they had no doubt forgotten—there had been developed in them a delicate, sensitive controlling mechanism that shut off their minds and emotions from all that the white race had said was taboo. Although they lived in an America where in theory there existed equality of opportunity, they knew unerringly what to aspire to and not to aspire to.

street corner for directions, and you may suddenly find yourself treated to a colorful history of your destination.

This hospitality is valued equally by black and white Mississippians. Many of the state's celebrated writers—including Eudora Welty and William Faulkner—have demonstrated in their work how this friendliness and respect can bring people from different backgrounds together, especially in times of conflict and hardship.

Mississippi authors have also demonstrated the dark side of their state's seductive friendliness and charm. Writers as diverse as the late playwright Tennessee Williams and contemporary novelist John Grisham have shown how polite words and friendly smiles can sometimes hide more troubling and complex feelings.

In most cases, however, the friendliness and civility are completely sincere and have a profound impact on the quality of life in Mississippi. Even in the state's few cities, visitors encounter a peaceful, small-town atmosphere that seems like a throwback to an earlier time. In small towns throughout the state, elderly men still greet one another in coat, hat, and tie at courthouse benches or along the town square. On the state's highways and back roads, farmers still look up from their machinery to wave at passing cars.

According to a young journalist in Oxford, this warmth and hospitality is what makes Mississippi so special to the people who live there. "I think what really sets Mississippi apart is the way people actually listen to each other," the young man explains, "Folks here really stop and take the time to hear what the other person is saying, even people who only know each other casually. To me, this gives Mississippi a certain closeness and intimacy that you don't find in other places, not even in other parts of the South."

Mississippians in Natchez loll away the afternoon.

RACE

If there is a single theme that unites and separates the people of Mississippi, it is the uneasy relationship between black Mississippians and white Mississippians. Mississippi has the second-lowest percentage of white residents (63 percent) and the highest percentage of black residents (36 percent) in the fifty states. All told, more than 99 percent of Mississippians are either black or white; less than one out of a hundred belong to any other group—by far the smallest number of any state.

A half-century ago, novelist William Faulkner described Mississippi's troubled history of racial relations with these now-famous words: "The past is never dead. It's not even past." Today, Faulkner's words still ring true. All across Mississippi, blacks and whites are still struggling to make sense of their state's painful history of injustice and racial conflict.

Some of the most heated conflicts have concerned the state's symbols. An ongoing debate in the state legislature regards the continued use of the Confederate "stars and crossed bars" in the present-day Mississippi flag. Opponents of the current flag explain that it is impossible for them to look at it and not be

ETHNIC MISSISSIPPI

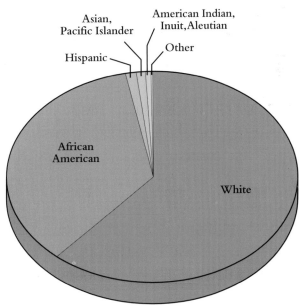

Asian, Pacific Islander

American Indian, Inuit, Aleutian

Other

Hispanic

African American

White

For future generations, the cotton plantations in the Mississippi Delta will be an ongoing reminder of the old system of slavery and racial oppression.

reminded of the suffering of black Mississippians under slavery—an injustice that the Confederacy was formed to defend. The flag's supporters contend that the old Confederate symbol represents both the best and the worst aspects of their state's past—both the injustice and white supremacy of the past, and the hospitality, civility, and honor in which Mississippians still take pride. "The whole thing is really confusing, and I don't see how we're ever going to resolve it to suit everybody," explains a student at Mississippi College who supports keeping the old flag. "I agree that there

THE GREEN CORN FESTIVAL

Each July, Mississippi Choctaws celebrate the Choctaw Indian Fair at their reservation in Neshoba County. The festival is modeled after the ancient Green Corn Festival, the most sacred day in the life of the Choctaws. Besides drawing crowds of locals and tourists, the festival also serves as a reunion for the Choctaws.

Participants in the original Green Corn Festival spent three to four days dancing and chanting to celebrate the harvest of their most important crop. Today, participants dress up in colorful traditional costumes to recreate the harvest dance and other traditional dances and social activities. Among the highlights are the animal dances—where Choctaws dance in costumes representing ducks, quails, snakes, and raccoons—and an annual stickball tournament.

Thousands of tourists visit Natchez to celebrate the customs and rituals of the pre–Civil War South.

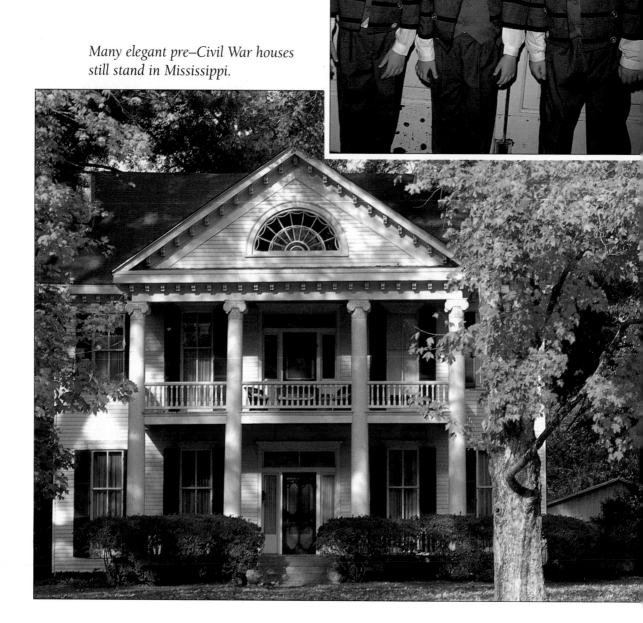

Many elegant pre–Civil War houses still stand in Mississippi.

At the Natchez Spring Pilgrimage, a small child proudly displays the clothing and manners of old Natchez.

are a lot of negative things about our flag—and the past history of our state, for that matter—but you can't just get rid of the flag. I mean, that's who we are, for better and for worse."

In the past few years, many black students at the University of Mississippi in Oxford have complained about the singing of "Dixie," a nostalgic ballad about the joys of plantation life, and the waving of the Confederate flag at the school's football games. In 1997, the student body senate banned all flags on poles at the games and discouraged students from bringing any Confederate flags into the stadium. Recently, the university's longtime mascot, an elderly white-haired gentleman named Colonel Rebel, has also been widely criticized. For an increasingly large number of students, the Colonel, whose costumes include a gray Confederate uniform, is no longer an appropriate symbol for a university that now welcomes African-American students and faculty.

It will probably be many years before black and white Mississippians find a common answer to these controversies. The feelings among both groups are much too strong to allow an easy solution. What both black and white Mississippians do agree about, however, is that more and more people in both groups are now committed to working together and finding solutions to their problems.

"Medgar Evers and James Meredith both said that if we ever turn the corner on race, Mississippi will be the best place to live," says David Sansing, a historian at the University of Mississippi. "We have turned the corner," he says. But sometimes, he adds, it seems like they're just going in a circle. "Maybe we'll get off of it one day. But at least we're in motion, and that's more than you can say for much of the country."

RELIGION

Religion plays an important part in the lives of most Mississippians. Located near the buckle of the Bible Belt, Mississippi has more churches per capita than any other state. Crowded together at the center of the state's towns, the tall steeples of stone sanctuaries seem to compete for the most prominent spot on the horizon. More modest churches, with green, well-shaded cemeteries in the back, are a frequent sight at major crossroads and on the outskirts of farm communities. Tiny one-roomed churches can also be found at the narrow entrances to backcountry roads, or on deeply rutted dirt roads in the middle of sprawling cotton plantations, often shaded by a single tree.

Christianity is the single dominant religion in Mississippi. Almost 95 percent of the state's residents identify themselves as Christian, the third-highest percentage of any state. Sunday mornings are a major social event, as families around the state dress in their nicest clothing to attend worship and then share a meal together at a favorite restaurant. "I always used to look forward to Sundays and church," recalls a former Mississippi resident who now lives in the Northeast. "It was the time when everyone came together—people whom you wouldn't normally see, or who didn't socialize during the rest of the week. Sundays in Mississippi are the one time when everything and everyone comes together."

Almost half of all Mississippians are Southern Baptists, by far the state's most powerful and vocal denomination. Southern Baptists have had an enormous impact on the state's social and cultural life. They have funded the development of major colleges and hospitals throughout the state and have taken a leading, usually conservative, role on important social issues. Methodists and Presbyterians are also well represented in Mississippi, particularly among whites.

African Americans belong to a wide variety of denominations, including Pentecostal Holiness, African Methodist-Episcopal, and a number of independent Baptist fellowships. The music and

From the Gulf Coast to the Delta, Mississippi's main streets and back roads are lined with churches.

preaching that can still be heard at the services of these small, emotionally charged congregations has had an enormous impact on the culture of both Mississippi and the entire nation.

During the late nineteenth and early twentieth centuries, black worshipers throughout the South mixed elements of Methodist hymn singing, white evangelical preaching, and African chanting and percussion to create a new form of music. Known today as gospel, this music combines the dark, mournful quality of the blues with the joyful exuberance of traditional Christian hymns. The powerful, sometimes frenzied sermons of Baptist and Pentecostal preachers have also influenced the performing styles of rock-and-roll and rhythm-and-blues musicians.

Like their deeply held religious beliefs, their commitment to hospitality, and their fondness for small-town life, Mississippians share a love of music. Together, these factors give the state a peaceful atmosphere—a way of life in which all Mississippians take pride.

5 THE BLUES AND BEYOND

The most significant achievements made by Mississippians have been in literature and music. Although Mississippi is a relatively small state, it has been the home of many of the nation's most celebrated writers and musicians. It is also the birthplace of one of the twentieth century's most important musical forms, the blues.

THE BIRTH OF THE BLUES

The music known as the blues began in the Mississippi Delta around the turn of the century. It was the music of black sharecroppers and the sons and daughters of freed slaves, combining African rhythms and field workers' call-and-response song style with dark, brooding singing. Its lyrics told the painful story of what it was like to be a poor black person in a world ruled by wealthy whites.

Among the many blues musicians born and raised in Mississippi are such legends as Charley Patton, Son House, Mississippi John Hurt, John Lee Hooker, Muddy Waters, Howlin' Wolf, Sonny Boy Williamson, and B. B. King. Robert Johnson was probably the most influential blues artist to claim Mississippi as his home. He was certainly the most mysterious. Born in 1911 in Hazelhurst, in southern Mississippi, he moved to the Delta town of Robinsonville when he was nine. As a boy, his favorite pastime was listening to

Though he only lived to be twenty-seven years old, Robert Johnson was the greatest of the Mississippi blues musicians. Many local people still believe that Johnson sold his soul to the devil in exchange for his extraordinary skill with the guitar.

the haunting music of the blues guitarists who played for spare change at the center of town. When Robert was in his teens, two of the Delta's most gifted blues musicians, Son House and Willie Brown, moved to Robinsonville, and Robert spent every free moment watching them play and trying to learn their techniques.

At first, the aspiring young guitarist showed little promise. Son House would later recall Johnson's earliest performances: "Such another racket you never heard! It'd make the people mad, you know. They'd come out and say, 'Why don't ya'll go in there and get the guitar away from that boy! He's running people crazy with it.'"

VICKSBURG BLUES

The blues is one of the great contributions made by African Americans to American and world culture. The cotton fields and levees of Mississippi have been among the most fertile areas for the growth of the blues.

Now, the rea-son I'm sing-in', my babe says she don't want me no more.

I've got those Vicksburg blues, and I'm singin' it everywhere I please.
I've got those Vicksburg blues, and I'm singin' it everywhere I please.
Now, the reason I'm singin', it is to give my poor heart ease.

Now, I don't like this place, mama, and I never will.
Now, I don't like this place, mama, and I never will.
I can sit right here in jail and look at Vicksburg on the hill.

When Son House, shown here performing in 1965, first heard Robert Johnson play, he couldn't believe how bad the young man was. "Don't do that, Robert," he told Johnson. "You drive people nuts. You can't play nothing."

One day, the young man became so frustrated by his failure to master the blues guitar that he ran away from home. No one knows for sure where he went or what he did while he was away, but when Johnson returned to Robinsonville six months later, he had somehow matured into an accomplished guitarist. He had developed a harsh, hypnotic style of playing and singing that was unlike anything local blues fans had ever heard before. "He was so good!" remembered Son House of Johnson's first public performance after his return. "When he finished, all our mouths were standing open."

Johnson was so good, in fact, that other jealous musicians began to spread the rumor that he had sold his soul to the devil in exchange for his extraordinary new skills. During the remaining years of his life, Johnson wrote and recorded some of the most remarkable songs in the history of American popular music. In brooding numbers like "Crossroad Blues" and "Hellhound on My Trail" he voiced the anger, suffering, and guilt that followed him throughout his life, and he helped define the blues as an art form.

Unfortunately, Johnson was never able to come to grips with the demons that haunted his personal life. He was a compulsive gambler and a heavy drinker and was frequently involved in fights. In 1938, Johnson was poisoned by the husband of a woman with whom he was having an affair. He was only twenty-seven years old.

THE KING OF ROCK AND ROLL

Mississippi's most famous resident, Elvis Presley, was born in a shack in Tupelo on January 8, 1935, the only child of Vernon and Gladys Presley. As a youngster, Elvis was fascinated by the different kinds of music that he heard around him. Listening to the radio he was introduced to spirited country music and popular ballads. At the small church that his family attended, he learned the slow hymns that he would love throughout his life. Elvis also enjoyed the faster, more explosive gospel songs that he heard through the thin walls of black churches. And he would sometimes spend hours listening to the dark, mournful blues songs played by old black men on Main Street in exchange for nickels and dimes.

When Elvis was thirteen, his family moved to Memphis, just over the Tennessee border. There Elvis first heard a new form of music called rock and roll. Rock and roll combined all the musical forms that Elvis enjoyed. It had the pure, exuberant joy of gospel; the hard, percussive power of the blues; the jangling rhythms of country; and the self-absorbed teenage romanticism of the day's popular ballads.

Elvis knew that he wanted to be a rock-and-roll musician. But at first, no one seemed interested in a white teenager who played and sang with the feverish intensity of a black blues singer. Then, when Elvis was nineteen, a local record producer named Sam Phillips invited him to a recording session with two of his best session musicians, guitarist Scotty Moore and bass player Bill Black.

At first, the session went badly. Elvis was shy and withdrawn in front of the older, more experienced musicians. Everything changed toward the end of the session, however, when Moore and Black began playing a popular blues tune called "That's All Right (Mama)." "All of a sudden," Scotty Moore would remember years later, "Elvis just started singing this song, jumping around and acting the fool, and then Bill picked up his bass, and he started acting the fool, too, and I started playing with them. Sam had the door to the control booth open, and he stuck head his out and said, 'What are you doing?' And we said, 'We don't know.' 'Well, back up,' he said, 'try to find a place to start, and do it again.'"

The song was released two weeks later and immediately became a hit in the area. By the end of the year, Elvis was the most popular young vocalist in the region, and his music was beginning to catch on among a national audience.

By 1956, Elvis had become the biggest selling recording artist in

Tupelo native Elvis Presley performs in 1956 with two members of his original backup band, guitarist Scotty Moore and bass player Bill Black. During the mid-1950s, Presley reigned as the undisputed King of Rock and Roll.

the history of American music. In a single week that summer, he had the number-one pop single ("I Want You, I Need You, I Love You"), the number-one rhythm-and-blues single ("Heartbreak Hotel"), and the number-one country single ("I Forgot to Remember to Forget"). By the time he was drafted into the army in 1958, Elvis had already sold more than 16 million records, including such classics as "Hound Dog," "Don't Be Cruel," and "Jailhouse Rock."

After his return from the army in 1960, Elvis released several hit singles, but failed to recapture the control of the music charts he had enjoyed during the 1950s. Instead, he starred in a series of successful movie musicals, including *Blue Hawaii* and *Viva Las Vegas*. In the early 1970s, he took his live act to Las Vegas, where he performed his old hits for old and new fans. When he died in 1977, at age forty-two, he was commonly regarded as the world's most popular entertainer.

THE FATHER OF COUNTRY MUSIC

Mississippi was also home to the man known as the Father of Country Music. Meridian resident Jimmie Rodgers worked for years as a brakeman for the railroads before he achieved fame as a country blues singer in the 1920s and 1930s, with such songs as "In the Jailhouse Now" and "Mule Skinner Blues." Rodgers had a distinc-

With his smooth southern charm and high falsetto yodel, Jimmie Rodgers was one of the most popular recording artists of the depression era. The subjects of his songs—loneliness, betrayal, and heartache—would become the standard themes of American country music.

tive, unforgettable singing style, ending the verses to many of his songs with a high-pitched yodel. He was a colorful character who continued to ride the rails and hang out with his old friends from the train yard throughout his life. When he died of tuberculosis in 1933, he was one of the nation's most popular recording artists, having sold more than 20 million records in the six years since his first single was released.

THE PRIDE OF THE PACKERS

Green Bay Packers quarterback Brett Favre was born and raised in the tiny town of Kiln. As a young boy, he often bragged to his coaches and classmates, "I'm going to quarterback in the Super

During the 1990s, Kiln native Brett Favre became a dominant player in the National Football League, leading the Green Bay Packers to the Super Bowl championship in 1997.

Bowl, and I'm going to win." Favre first gained national recognition as a college standout at the University of Southern Mississippi. After joining the Green Bay Packers in 1992, he rapidly matured into one of the National Football League's best players—and the league's most respected and feared quarterback.

In 1995, Favre won the first of his three NFL Most Valuable Player awards. Two years later, Favre made his childhood prediction come true, leading the Packers to a 35–21 Super Bowl victory over the New England Patriots.

A CIVIL RIGHTS PIONEER

Years before the civil rights movement of the 1950s and 1960s, Holly Springs native Ida Bell Wells took a bold stand for the rights

Ida Bell Wells became famous for her blunt and passionate protests against lynching.

of African Americans in Mississippi and around the nation. A journalist and social reformer, she was a founding member of the National Association for the Advancement of Colored People (NAACP), one of the first groups to seek equal rights for African Americans. An editor and part owner of *Free Speech*, a Memphis, Tennessee, newspaper, she wrote dozens of fiery articles during the late nineteenth and early twentieth centuries denouncing lynching and other social ills. She also worked organizing black women to protest discriminatory laws and practices. She continued to crusade for justice until her death in 1931.

THE NOBEL PRIZE–WINNER

The state's most celebrated author, William Cuthbert Faulkner, was born September 25, 1897, in the small town of New Albany. Shortly before William's fifth birthday, the Faulkners moved to Oxford. As a child, William fell in love with the peaceful town, with its proud old courthouse on the town square and its hilly, tree-lined streets. Though he would travel extensively as an adult, Oxford would remain Faulkner's home.

Although Faulkner's first few novels were well received, it was his 1929 novel *The Sound and the Fury* that established him as one of the world's most important young authors. The novel was experimental for its time. It told the same story from the point of view of different characters in one family, including a mentally retarded adult. During the next ten years, Faulkner produced what is arguably the most impressive body of work of any writer in U.S. history, including his great novels *As I Lay Dying, Sanctuary, Light in*

William Faulkner is considered one of the greatest writers of the twentieth century.

August, Absalom, Absalom! and *The Wild Palms*. Many of Faulkner's works describe the troubled but colorful lives of the inhabitants of the imaginary Yoknapatawpha County. Life in Yoknapatawpha bore a striking resemblance to life in Oxford's Lafayette County.

Although they earned critical acclaim, Faulkner's works never sold many copies. Faced with mounting debt during the 1940s, he turned to writing screenplays to support himself. In Hollywood, he wrote some of the era's finest motion pictures, including *To Have and Have Not* and *The Big Sleep*.

In 1949, Faulkner was awarded the Nobel Prize for literature, the most prestigious prize a writer can win. In his stirring acceptance speech, he summed up the values expressed throughout his fiction. "I believe that man will not merely survive," Faulkner declared. "He will prevail."

Faulkner's novels set the standard for the gifted group of Mississippi writers who followed, including Eudora Welty, Tennessee Williams, Margaret Walker Alexander, Richard Wright, and Walker Percy. Today, Faulkner's hometown of Oxford is the center of the state's ongoing literary tradition. Several of the South's most celebrated authors—among them Willie Morris, Barry Hannah, and Larry Brown—live in the town, many of them teaching a new generation of Mississippi writers at the local university.

On September 25, 1997, the hundredth anniversary of Faulkner's birth, a life-size statue of the author was unveiled in the town square. In what resembled a scene from one of Faulkner's own novels, many of Oxford's residents argued passionately over the city's decision to cut down a favorite old magnolia tree to make room for the statue.

6 CITIES AND SMALL TOWNS

Mississippi is primarily a rural state. On the state's highways, motorists spend most of their time observing forests and farmland and fields full of wildflowers. For those who follow the occasional signs leading off the highway, however, the state offers a surprising number of landmarks and historical sites.

THE NORTH

Tupelo, in Mississippi's northeast hill country, is known primarily as the birthplace of rock-and-roll pioneer Elvis Presley. The two-room house where Presley was born is located on a quiet, tree-lined street on the outskirts of town. On the hill behind the house sits a tiny chapel, along with a small visitors center and gift shop.

Forty-five minutes west of Tupelo is the town of Oxford. The home of the University of Mississippi, the Center for the Study of Southern Culture, and the University's Blues Archive, Oxford is one of the South's leaders in music and literature—both past and present. At the center of town, Square Books offers browsers one of the finest collections of southern literature in the country. The coffee shop on the bookstore's second floor is a favorite meeting place for university students, literary buffs, and local writers.

Just a short walk from the town square, visitors can stroll among the magnolia trees, pines, and tall cedars that provide the shade for

Rowan Oak, the stately home of novelist William Faulkner, sits hidden behind a wall of cedar trees, just a short walk from Oxford's downtown square.

Rowan Oak, the stately white house in which celebrated author William Faulkner spent much of his adult life. On one wall, visitors can see the place where Faulkner, who had run out of paper, once scribbled the outline for one of his novels. Faulkner is buried at the edge of a large, peaceful cemetery not far from Rowan Oak.

THE MISSISSIPPI DELTA

As you drive west of Oxford, the northern hills gradually empty out into the flat, seemingly endless farmland of the Mississippi Delta. Most of the Delta is covered by enormous cotton fields and plan-

Although Mississippi is best known for its huge cotton plantations, many of the state's farmers work fields of only a few acres, storing their modest crops in barns and simple wooden sheds.

tations. The relation between wealth and poverty in the area is star-tling. The majestic mansions of wealthy planters rise proudly out of the same fields that contain the tiny, dilapidated wooden shacks of the people who work the fields.

Depending on the season, huge harvesting combines or long, odd-looking irrigation systems are scattered here and there across the fields. During the late harvesting season, the pure, ripe cotton bolls stretch out as far as the eye can see, like a white, fluffy sea against the pale blue, sun-bleached horizon. The region's few trees jut out occasionally from creek beds and marshes and line the paved entrances to the stately plantation homes.

Beside the one-bench railroad stop in the tiny Delta town of Tutwiler, a large plaque commemorates the spot where the great African-American composer W. C. Handy first heard the mournful sound of the blues in 1903. In the years that followed, Handy would incorporate the blues into many of his most popular songs, such as "St. Louis Blues," which introduced people around the world to this vital new form of music. A colorful mural on the opposite side of the railroad tracks, by local artists Cristen Craven Barnard and Hubert Murphy, depicts the scene in which the well-dressed composer, his hat in his hands, listens attentively to the strange sounds made by a local musician.

The mural reads: "In 1903, while touring in the Delta and playing musical engagements, W. C. Handy was waiting for a train in Tutwiler. At the train depot, an unknown musician was singing, while sliding a knife blade down the strings of his guitar. The sound and effect were unforgettable to Handy and became the music known worldwide as 'The Blues.'"

On a back road south of Tutwiler, beside a run-down, wood-framed church building, is the grave of the great blues singer and harmonica player Aleck Miller, popularly known as Sonny Boy Williamson. Williamson's tombstone is at the back of a tiny, over-grown cemetery. The rusty harmonicas that litter the grave site were left as tributes by blues fans and aspiring musicians.

Near the center of the Delta, the city of Clarksdale is the site of the Delta Blues Museum. Housed on the second floor of the local library, the museum contains many rare blues artifacts, including one of B. B. King's original guitars, a steel-bodied acoustic guitar once owned by Son House, and a life-size wax figure of Muddy Waters. The museum is committed to "preserving, protecting and perpetuating the Blues," and often hosts classes taught by local blues musicians in blues history and playing techniques.

VICKSBURG

Perched on high bluffs overlooking the Mississippi River is the historic port city of Vicksburg. The site of the siege of Vicksburg, one of the most important battles of the Civil War, the city is the home of the largest Civil War cemetery in the United States. The Vicksburg National Military Park preserves the rolling grass-covered hills and deep ravines where thousands of Union and Confederate soldiers clashed during the bloody battles of General Grant's two-month blockade of the city. Today, motorists drive a sixteen-mile tour of the battleground, lined by hundreds of statues, monuments, and plaques commemorating battle sites and the various state units that took part in the fighting. Before and after park hours each day, joggers and hikers turn the winding roadway into a popular exercise route and meeting place.

NATCHEZ

The largest port city in southwestern Mississippi, Natchez is one of the most beautiful and historically rich cities in the United

TEN LARGEST CITIES

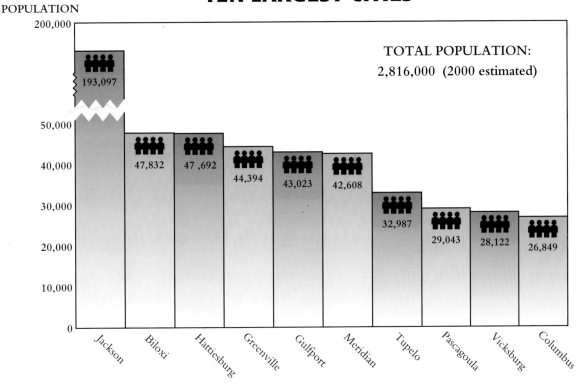

POPULATION

TOTAL POPULATION:
2,816,000 (2000 estimated)

200,000

193,097

50,000

47,832   47,692

44,394   43,023   42,608

40,000

30,000

32,987

29,043   28,122   26,849

20,000

10,000

0

Jackson Biloxi Hattiesburg Greenville Gulfport Meridian Tupelo Pascagoula Vicksburg Columbus

States. It has more than six hundred pre–Civil War homes— the most of any southern city. More than one hundred of these magnificent, antebellum (pre–Civil War) structures are registered historic landmarks, and many can be toured. During Christmas-time, all of Natchez's historic homes are opened to the public. Highlights of the tour include Stanton Hall, a magnificent white palace with two-story columns, which was built in 1857; and Longwood, an octagonal brick home with an oriental-style dome.

Known as the City of Azaleas, Natchez's sidewalks and yards

Cannons, statues, and monuments line the green rolling hills of the huge military cemetery in Vicksburg, the site of one of the most important battles of the Civil War.

are densely lined with azaleas, magnolias, dogwoods, and other flowering trees and shrubs. For visitors who would prefer not to brave the Mississippi heat on foot, horse-drawn carriages, red double-decker buses, and green-and-brown trolley cars carry visitors up and down the city's historic stretch.

WE PUT THE COKE IN THE BOTTLE

In 1894, customers at the Biedenharn Candy Company, in Vicksburg, became the first people in the world to be served Coca-Cola in bottles. Today, the site of the original bottling works has been remodeled as the Biedenharn Museum of Coca-Cola History and Memorabilia. The museum features restored bottling equipment from the turn of the century and an old-fashioned soda fountain. Museum visitors can sample both the more syrupy, carbonated Coca-Cola that was popular in the days before bottling and today's recipe in original-size, ice-cold bottles.

Down the hill from the antebellum home district is the historic nineteenth-century flatboat and steamboat landing area known as Natchez Under-the-Hill. The hillside offers a spectacular view of the Mississippi River and the dense greenery of the Louisiana countryside across the way.

A few miles north of Natchez, Emerald Mound, the region's largest surviving Indian mound, is a startling sight. Shaped like a pyramid, it is more than six hundred feet long and four hundred feet wide and covers almost six acres of the lush, green countryside.

JACKSON

The capital city of Jackson is a peaceful, tree-lined community of approximately 200,000 inhabitants. At first glance, it looks more like an overgrown village than a thriving city. Near the capitol building at the center of town, businesspeople and government workers stroll leisurely to and from their offices. People frequently pause to chat with friends on street corners, or to drink coffee and read the morning paper in one of the many small diners and cafés. But despite its sleepy appearance, Jackson is one of the Deep South's centers of art, architecture, health care, and education.

At the center of town, several of the state's finest buildings are scattered along a six-block stretch. Modeled after the national capitol building in Washington, D.C., the state capitol—called the New Capitol—is a huge, three-story brick structure. The New Capitol's

Each Christmas in Natchez, all of the city's historic antebellum homes are opened to the public.

REMEMBERING MEDGAR EVERS

Away from Jackson's downtown, the Medgar Evers Home is now open to the public as a historical landmark. Located in a low-income, predominantly African-American neighborhood on the outskirts of town, the home is where the respected civil rights leader was assassinated by Byron de la Beckwith on June 12, 1963.

In the same part of Jackson, on nearby Medgar Evers Boulevard, is the Medgar Evers Memorial Statue. The five-hundred-pound, cast-bronze statue shows Evers standing with his arms crossed, in a hopeful but defiant position. It is a familiar posture for those who knew the man. "That's Medgar all right," an older black man explained to his young grandson as they approached the statue. In the statue, Evers is looking east toward Jackson, the city where he fought so stubbornly and courageously for equal rights and opportunities for African Americans. The inscription at the base of the statue presents the simple message:

Dedicated to Everyone
Who Believes in Peace
Love and Non-Violence
Let's Keep the Torch Burning.

tall, white columns rise proudly above the arched doorways on the first floor. Only a few blocks away, its well-preserved predecessor, the Old Capitol, is one of America's finest examples of Greek Revival architecture. A striking white building, the Old Capitol is made entirely of limestone, granite, and marble. A majestic golden eagle sits atop its massive copper dome. Since the early 1960s, it has served as a state historical museum.

The capital city of Jackson is the state's largest metropolitan area.

Not far from the capitol, Hal and Mal's, a popular rib house, offers a glimpse of another side of Jackson. Each night, young people crowd into the building to hear the South's leading blues, rhythm-and-blues, and rock-and-roll musicians. All along the restaurant's walls are signed photographs of respected blues musicians—such as B. B. King, Muddy Waters, and John Lee Hooker—who played at the club in the past. "It's just great to see young people coming out together to hear this music," says manager Malcolm White. "That's why I do this. We're known for the blues here, but, the truth is, we get every kind of music. People down here really love their music."

MERIDIAN

Meridian is the largest city in the eastern part of the state. The city was once an important railroad center for the Deep South, serving as a hub for train traffic to and from the industrial and tourist centers of the South, such as Memphis, Birmingham, New Orleans, Atlanta, and Mobile.

At Highland Park in Meridian, the Jimmie Rodgers Museum allows visitors a chance to learn more about the life and music of the Father of Country Music and the railroad era that he memorialized in song. In addition to the singer's guitar and the furniture from his home, the museum also boasts an entire steam engine.

THE GULF COAST

Each night, the bright neon lights of gambling casinos and high-rise hotels dominate Mississippi's once-peaceful coastline. Despite the area's recent development, however, the Gulf Coast is still the home of some of the state's most enduring symbols of the Confederacy and the Old South. Fort Massachusetts, completed just after the Civil War, is preserved as a war memorial on West Ship Island, off the shore of Gulfport, and the 150-year-old Biloxi Lighthouse still stands defiantly in the middle of the four-lane highway that runs along the shore.

Folk singer and railroad worker Jimmie Rodgers is generally regarded as the Father of Country Music. Rodgers's life and music are commemorated at the Jimmie Rodgers Memorial Museum in Meridian, the singer's hometown.

The area's most frequently visited historical landmark is Beauvoir, the large antebellum mansion where Confederate president Jefferson Davis spent his last years. The mansion and grounds have been completely restored and serve as a memorial to Davis and the Confederacy.

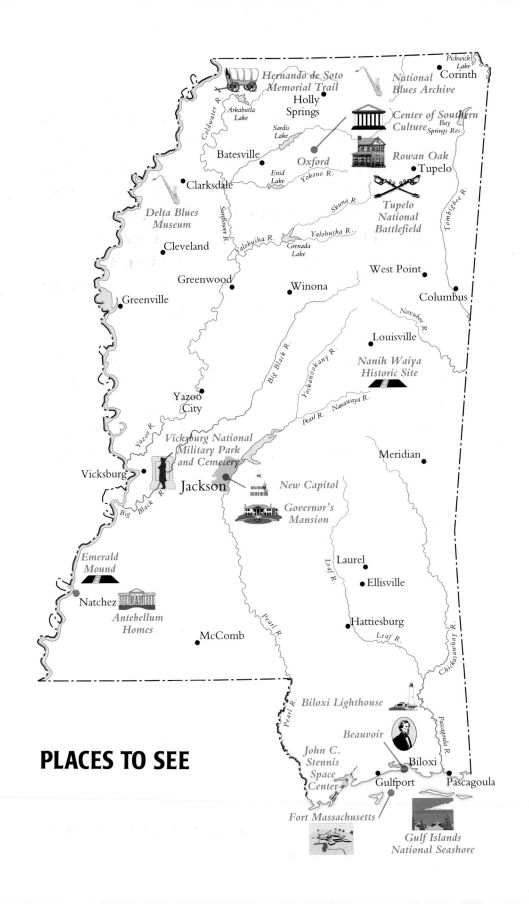

Pickwick Lake

Corinth

Hernando de Soto Memorial Trail

National Blues Archive

Holly Springs

Center of Southern Culture

Bay Springs Res.

Coldwater R.

Arkabutla Lake

Sardis Lake

Batesville

Oxford

Rowan Oak

Tupelo

Enid Lake

Yokono R.

Clarksdale

Skuna R.

Tombigbee R.

Delta Blues Museum

Sunflower R.

Yalobusha R.

Yalobusha R.

Tupelo National Battlefield

Grenada Lake

Cleveland

West Point

Greenwood

Winona

Columbus

Greenville

Noxubee R.

Louisville

Big Black R.

Yakanookany R.

Nanih Waiya Historic Site

Yazoo City

Pearl R.

Nanawaya R.

Yazoo R.

Vicksburg National Military Park and Cemetery

Meridian

Vicksburg

Big Black R.

Jackson

New Capitol

Governor's Mansion

Emerald Mound

Leaf R.

Laurel

Ellisville

Natchez

Antebellum Homes

McComb

Pearl R.

Hattiesburg

Leaf R.

Chickasawhay R.

Pearl R.

Biloxi Lighthouse

Beauvoir

Pascagoula R.

PLACES TO SEE

John C. Stennis Space Center

Biloxi

Gulfport

Pascagoula

Fort Massachusetts

Gulf Islands National Seashore

Not surprisingly, black and white Mississippians often have very different reactions to the historical information and memorabilia housed at Beauvoir and other monuments to the Old South. More and more, citizens have learned to express their differences openly, and discussions of the state's troubled racial history can sometimes be heard among groups visiting the museum. "I tell you the truth," admitted an African-American teacher from Biloxi, who had just led her racially mixed sixth-grade class on a tour of the Davis home. "I was offended at first when the school said they wanted me to bring my class here."

"But the kids were curious about the place," she continued. "They're open about asking questions—to me, to the tour guide, to each other. And I think maybe that's the best thing. To have all these black children and white children learning about the past together. Asking questions and making it their own history, their own shared story."

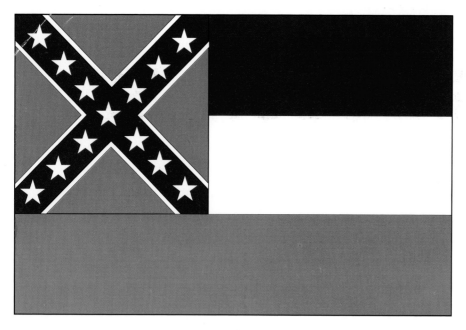

THE FLAG: *The state flag has three broad horizontal bars of blue, white, and red. In the upper left-hand corner is the Confederate flag, a blue cross outlined in white with thirteen stars, all on a red background. The flag was adopted in 1894.*

THE SEAL: *Adopted in 1894, the state seal features an eagle with outstretched wings. It holds an olive branch in its right talon and three arrows in its left. Encircling the seal are the words "The Great Seal of the State of Mississippi."*

STATE SURVEY

Statehood: December 10, 1817

Origin of Name: From the Native American word *misi-sipi*, meaning "big river" or "father of waters"

Nickname: Magnolia State

Capital: Jackson

Motto: By Valor and Arms

Bird: Mockingbird

Waterfowl: Wood duck

Land Mammal: White-tailed deer

Water Mammal: Bottle-nosed dolphin

Fish: Largemouth or black bass

Flower: Magnolia

Mockingbird

Magnolia

GO, MISSISSIPPI

"Go, Mississippi" was adopted as the official state song of the Magnolia State by the legislature on May 17, 1962.

By Houston Davis

Go, Mis - si - sip - pi, keep roll - ing a - long,———

Go, Mis - sis - sip - pi, you can - not go wrong.———

Go, Mis - sis - sip - pi, we're sing - ing your song:———

M - I - S, - S - I - S, - S - I - P - P - I.

Wildflower: Coreopsis

Tree: Magnolia

Insect: Honeybee

Stone: Petrified wood

Fossil: Prehistoric whale

Shell: Oyster shell

Dance: Square dance

Beverage: Milk

GEOGRAPHY

Highest Point: 806 feet above sea level, at Woodall Mountain

Lowest Point: Sea level, along the Gulf of Mexico

Area: 47,233 square miles

Greatest Distance, North to South: 330 miles

Greatest Distance, East to West: 190 miles

Bordering States: Alabama to the east, Tennessee to the north, Arkansas and Louisiana to the west

Hottest Recorded Temperature: 115°F at Holly Springs on July 29, 1930

Coldest Recorded Temperature: -19°F at Corinth on January 30, 1966

Average Annual Precipitation: 56 inches

Major Rivers: Big Black, Chickasawhay, Leaf, Mississippi, Pascagoula, Pearl, Tallahatchie, Yazoo

Major Lakes: Arkabutla, Columbus, Enid, Grenada, Okatibbee, Ross Barnett, Sardis

Trees: black oak, cottonwood, cypress, hickory, live oak, magnolia, pecan, pine, red oak, tupelo, walnut

Wild Plants: azalea, black-eyed Susan, dogwood, redbud, violet

Animals: black bear, bobcat, coyote, fox, opossum, rabbit, raccoon, squirrel, white-tailed deer, woodchuck

Birds: duck, goose, mockingbird, mourning dove, quail, wild turkey

Fish: bream, catfish, flounder, largemouth bass, marlin, mullet, perch, redfish

Endangered Animals: American burying beetle, Atlantic Ridley tortoise, Bachman's warbler, bald eagle, black clubshell mussel, brown pelican, fat pocketbook mussel, Florida panther, gray bat, hawksbill turtle, Indiana bat, ivory-billed woodpecker, least tern, leatherback turtle, Mississippi sandhill crane, ovate clubshell mussel, pallid sturgeon, peregrine falcon, red-cockaded woodpecker, southern clubshell mussel, southern combshell mussel, southern pink pigtoe mussel, southern round pigtoe mussel, stirrup shell mussel, West Indian manatee

West Indian manatee

Endangered Plants: American chaffseed, Pondberry spicebush, Price's
potato bean

TIMELINE

Mississippi History

1500s Choctaw, Chickasaw, and Natchez Indians live in present-day
Mississippi

1540 Spanish explorer Hernando de Soto is the first European to reach
Mississippi

1682 René-Robert Cavelier, Sieur de La Salle, claims Mississippi for France

1699 Pierre Le Moyne of France establishes Fort Maurepas at Old Biloxi,
the first European settlement in Mississippi

1719 The French bring the first African slaves to Mississippi to work on rice
and tobacco plantations

1763 As a result of its victory in the French and Indian War, Britain
acquires Mississippi from France

1798 The Mississippi Territory is created with Natchez as its capital

1806 A new variety of cotton is introduced to Mississippi from Mexico,
beginning the Great Cotton Era

1817 Mississippi becomes the 20th state

1821 The state capital moves to Jackson

1830 Choctaw Indians sign the Dancing Rabbit Creek Treaty, giving up their lands in Mississippi

1861 Mississippi secedes from the Union as the Civil War begins

1862 Jefferson Davis, a former U.S. senator from Mississippi, becomes president of the Confederacy

1863 General Ulysses S. Grant captures Vicksburg during the Civil War, giving the North control of the Mississippi River

1868 A new state constitution gives African Americans in Mississippi the right to vote and hold elected office

1870 Mississippi is readmitted to the Union

1871 The state opens Alcorn University, the first state-supported college for African Americans in the United States

1890 Mississippi adopts a new state constitution that takes away many of the rights given to African Americans in the previous constitution

1926 The state becomes one of the first to ban the teaching of evolution in its public schools

1939 Oil is discovered in Yazoo County, marking the beginning of the oil industry in Mississippi

1949 Mississippian William Faulkner wins the Nobel Prize in literature

1962 Despite protests and riots, James Meredith becomes the first African-American student at the University of Mississippi; federal troops arrive in Mississippi to maintain order

1963 Civil rights leader Medgar Evers is assassinated at his home in Jackson

1964 New federal civil rights laws force Mississippi to integrate its public schools

1973 Eudora Welty wins the Pulitzer Prize in fiction for her novel *The Optimist's Daughter*

1986 Mike Espy is the first African American elected to the U.S. House of Representatives from Mississippi

1988 Eugene Marino, a native of Biloxi, becomes the first African-American Roman Catholic archbishop in the United States

Cotton bolls

ECONOMY

Agricultural Products: beef, cotton, eggs, milk, poultry, rice, soybeans

Manufactured Products: bricks, chemicals, clothing, electronic equipment, fertilizers, paper, processed foods, ships, wood products

Natural Resources: bauxite, limestone, lumber, natural gas, oil, salt

Business and Trade: banking, insurance, investment securities, public finance, retail sales

CALENDAR OF CELEBRATIONS

Martin Luther King Day On Martin Luther King Day in January, towns throughout the state host parades, lectures, seminars, and other activities to honor the memory of the great civil rights leader.

Dixie National Livestock Show and Rodeo This is the second-largest livestock show and largest rodeo east of the Mississippi River. Held each year in February in Jackson, it features several weeks of livestock competitions and rodeo events.

Gulf Coast History Week Celebrated in February in Biloxi, this event gives visitors a glimpse at Mississippi's 18th-century French heritage. The weeklong celebration features re-creations of colonial French homes and demonstrations of early crafts.

Mardi Gras Parade and Ball Each year prior to the beginning of Lent, the period before Easter, the people of Natchez celebrate Mardi Gras with music, parades, costume balls, and other festivities.

Natchez Powwow At the end of March, Native Americans from around the United States gather in Natchez to celebrate their heritage. Activities include dancing, music, and crafts demonstrations.

Vicksburg Spring Pilgrimage Visitors to Vicksburg in the spring get a chance to visit beautiful homes from the period before the Civil War. People can tour the houses and their gardens and ride riverboats to relive a bygone era.

World Catfish Festival In April Belzoni celebrates the world's largest catfish fry. Activities include arts-and-crafts exhibits, music and dancing, and the crowning of the Catfish Queen.

Fort Maurepas d'Iberville reenactment

Natchez Opera Festival From April to June classical-music lovers flock to Natchez to hear performances of opera and Broadway shows.

Blessing of the Fleet This colorful event, held in Biloxi each May, celebrates the beginning of the fishing season. Fishermen and their boats gather in the harbor to receive a religious blessing before venturing out into the Gulf of Mexico.

Mississippi Arts Fair for the Handicapped Held in Biloxi in early June, this three-day event provides an opportunity for disabled citizens to share in music, dance, and drama events.

Fireworks Extravaganza This Fourth of July celebration at Robinsonville features one of the largest fireworks displays in the Southeast.

Neshoba County Fair Held in August and known as Mississippi's Giant Houseparty, this annual fair has been celebrated since 1889. One of the last remaining old-style county fairs in the South, it features dancing, singing, horse racing, and other types of entertainment.

Mississippi State Fair Held in Biloxi each September, the state fair is the largest in the South. In addition to traditional livestock shows, the fair offers educational demonstrations, art exhibits, entertainment, and carnival rides.

Magnolia State Fall Bluegrass Festival Each October visitors to Wiggins are treated to some of the best bluegrass music heard anywhere in the nation. The event is one of the South's most popular music festivals.

Christmas on the Water In early December, Biloxi starts the Christmas season with a children's parade, boat parade, and other festivities.

STATE STARS

Blanche Kelso Bruce (1841–1898), was the second African American to serve in the U.S. Senate. Bruce was born in Virginia and moved to Mississippi in 1869. In 1874, he was elected to the U.S. Senate, where he devoted much of his time to fighting corruption and promoting better race relations. After leaving the Senate, Bruce served in the U.S. Treasury Department.

Blanche Kelso Bruce

Bo Diddley (1928–   ), a well-known rhythm-and-blues singer, was born Elias McDaniel in McComb. A self-taught musician,

Bo Diddley

the African-American singer gained fame for the driving tempo of his music. A pioneer of the electric guitar, he became one of the first rock-and-roll stars with songs such as "Who Do You Love?"

Medgar Evers (1925–1963), born in Decatur, was one of the best-known civil rights leaders of the 1950s and early 1960s. He joined the NAACP in 1952 and later became secretary for the organization in Mississippi. He played an important role in the struggle to end segregation in Mississippi, giving fiery speeches about the rights of African Americans. Because of his outspoken position, Evers became a target for civil rights opponents. In 1963 he was assassinated by Byron de la Beckwith.

William Faulkner (1897–1962), one of the greatest American writers of the 20th century, was born in New Albany. Faulkner spent most of his career in Mississippi writing about the South. In his books, which reflect the color and history of the region, he explores love, bravery, and endurance. Faulkner won the Nobel Prize in literature in 1949 and the Pulitzer Prize in 1955 and 1963 for his novels *A Fable* and *The Reivers*.

John Grisham (1955–   ), a popular novelist, was born in Arkansas but grew up in Mississippi. Originally a lawyer, Grisham was inspired to write by a trial he watched in 1984. His first novel, *A Time to Kill*, got good reviews but sold few copies. However, his next novel, *The Firm*, became a best-seller and launched his career. Many of his books have been made into movies, including *The Firm*, *The Pelican Brief*, and *The Client*.

John Grisham

Fannie Lou Hamer (1917–1977), a civil rights leader, was born to sharecroppers in Montgomery County. She became active in the civil rights movement, organizing protests, leading voter-registration drives, and working to reform the Democratic Party so that African Americans were treated fairly.

Beth Henley (1952–   ), a playwright, was born in Jackson. Henley is best known for witty comedies and emotional dramas that highlight the atmosphere of the South. Henley first pursued a career in acting, but she turned to writing plays after discovering that there were not many good roles for southern women. Her first play, *Crimes of the Heart*, won a Tony Award and a Pulitzer Prize in 1981.

Jim Henson (1936–1990), the creator of the Muppets, was born in Greenville. Henson began working as a puppeteer, but he really wanted a career in television. In 1955 his puppet creations appeared on a local television station in Maryland. In 1969 Henson and his Muppets became a household name when *Sesame Street* first appeared on television. The Muppets—including Big Bird, Bert, Ernie, Miss Piggy, and Kermit the Frog—became the beloved friends of millions of kids around the world.

Jim Henson

James Earl Jones (1931–   ), a well-known African-American actor, was born in Arkabutla. Best known for his deep, rumbling voice, Jones has appeared in many movies and on television. In one of his most famous roles he did not even appear onscreen, but was the voice of Darth Vader in the *Star Wars* movies. He also appeared in the television miniseries *Roots* and in the movie *Field of Dreams*. A stage actor as well, Jones won a Tony Award in 1969 for his role in *The Great White Hope*.

B. B. King (1925–   ), a legendary blues singer and guitarist, was born in Itta Bena. His singing style combines gospel and the blues. His music, including innovative guitar playing, became a model for many blues performers in the late 1960s.

B. B. King

James Meredith (1933–   ), born in Kosciusko, gained fame in 1962 as the first African American to attend the University of Mississippi. In 1966 he led a civil rights march from Memphis, Tennessee, to Jackson, Mississippi, to encourage African Americans to register to vote. During the march Meredith was shot and wounded, but he rejoined the march after recovering from his wounds. He ran unsuccessfully for the U.S. Senate in 1972.

Brandy Norwood (1979–   ), born in McComb, is better known as Brandy. The popular singer and actress recorded her first album at age 14. Two singles from that album, "I Wanna Be Down" and "Baby," became hits. Her singing style combines rhythm and blues, gospel, and soul music. In 1993 she landed a role on the television program *Thea* and went on to star in the show *Moesha*, which premiered in 1995.

Walter Payton (1954–   ), born in Columbia, is one of the greatest running backs in football history. After being named an All-American at Jackson State University, he began his professional career with the Chicago Bears in 1975. He led the NFL in rushing every year from 1975 to 1979 and was named player of the year in 1977. Payton retired in 1987.

Elvis Presley (1935–1977), one of the great legends of American music, was born in Tupelo. The singer combined country and western with rhythm and blues to help define the new sound of rock and roll. Songs such as "Heartbreak Hotel," "Love Me Tender," and "Don't Be Cruel" made him one of the most popular performers of the 1950s and 1960s. Although his life was cut short, his music and popularity have endured.

Leontyne Price (1927–   ), one of the world's most famous African-America opera singers, was born in Laurel. The soprano has sung in most of the major opera houses of the world, including the Metropolitan Opera in New York City. She is best known for her dramatic roles in operas such as *Aida* and *Il Trovatore*. Now retired from the opera stage, Price still gives occasional recitals and teaches.

Leontyne Price

Charley Pride (1938–   ), the first well-known African-American country singer, was born on a cotton plantation in Sledge. As a young man, Pride taught himself to play guitar but hoped for a career in professional baseball. After playing in the minor leagues for about 10 years, he decided to become a singer and set out for Nashville, where his initial success came with appearances on the Grand Ole Opry.

Pushmataha (1765?–1824), a Choctaw Indian chief, was born near Noxuba Creek. In the early 1800s, he began working to ensure peace between his tribe and the U.S. government. In 1805 Pushmataha signed a treaty that allowed white settlement on Choctaw land. Later, he persuaded his tribe to join the United States in fighting against the Creek Indians in the Creek War. In 1816 and 1820 he signed other agreements with the U.S. government, giving away more of the Indians' lands.

Hiram Rhodes Revels (1827–1901), though born in North Carolina, served Mississippi as the first African-American member of the U.S. Senate. He settled in Natchez in 1866 and was elected to the state senate. In 1870 he was chosen to fill an unexpired term in the U.S. Senate. As a senator, Revels sought to improve the education of African Americans. He served only one term and then became president of Alcorn University in Mississippi, a college for African Americans.

Hiram Rhodes Revels

Jerry Rice (1962–   ), a professional football player, was born in Starkville. An All-American at Mississippi Valley State, Rice joined the San Francisco

49ers in 1985. He soon earned a reputation as the best wide receiver in professional football. He led the league in yardage and touchdowns in 1986 and set many records in the following years. Rice played with the 49ers in two Super Bowl championships and was named Most Valuable Player in the 1989 game.

Pearl Rivers (1849–1896), born Elizabeth Jane Poitevent in Hancock County, was the first woman publisher of an important daily newspaper. Writing under the name Pearl Rivers, she became an editor of the *New Orleans Times-Picayune* in 1870. She married the owner of the paper and managed it herself after his death in 1876, adding sections for women, such as fashion and household tips, and a society page.

Jimmie Rodgers (1897–1933), known as the Father of Country Music, was born in Meridian. He taught himself to play the guitar and banjo and developed a singing style that combined country, blues, and cowboy music. Rodgers became a popular recording artist and toured throughout the South. His songs, including such hits as "Brakeman's Blues" and "Mississippi River Blues," had a great influence on other singers.

Conway Twitty (1933–   ), a country singer and guitarist, was born in Friars Point with the name Harold Jenkins. Twitty made his first radio appearance at age 10. He recorded his first hits, including "I Need Your Lovin'," in 1958. Since the 1970s Twitty has appeared regularly at the Grand Ole Opry, often paired with singer Loretta Lynn.

Muddy Waters (1915–1983), a legendary African-American blues singer, was born McKinley Morganfield in Rolling Fork. He began his professional singing career in 1943 after moving to Chicago and became known as King of the Chicago Blues. His unique style, which sounded like moaning and shouting, influenced many rhythm-and-blues bands, especially in England. One of his songs, "Rollin' Stone," served as inspiration for the English group the Rolling Stones.

Ida Bell Wells (1862–1931), a journalist, was born to slave parents in Holly Springs. Wells taught in rural schools before becoming a journalist in the 1880s. In 1892 Wells began a crusade to stop lynching in the South, traveling throughout the United States and England speaking to anti-lynching societies. In 1910 she founded the Chicago Negro Fellowship League, which helped African Americans who had migrated from the South. She also played a role in founding the NAACP.

Eudora Welty (1909–   ), a well-known writer, was born in Jackson. Throughout her career, Welty's work has focused on Mississippi and its people. Her writings paint a colorful and vibrant portrait of life in the South. In the 1930s Welty had essays published in literary reviews. Some short stories, published in the 1940s, brought her great success. She won the Pulitzer Prize in 1973 for her novel *The Optimist's Daughter*.

Eudora Welty

Tennessee Williams (1911–1983), one of America's greatest playwrights, was born Thomas Lanier Williams in Columbus. In 1938 he went to New Orleans and began using the name "Tennessee" on stories he wrote for magazines. He first gained fame as a playwright in the 1940s and won

the Pulitzer Prize in 1948 and 1955 for his plays *A Streetcar Named Desire* and *Cat on a Hot Tin Roof*. His works—noted for their realism, intense emotions, and use of symbolism—are classics of the theater.

Tennessee Williams

Oprah Winfrey (1954–   ), a popular television talk-show host, was born in Kosciusko. After winning two beauty pageants, she went to college at Tennessee State University and then landed a job on a local television news program. In 1983 she got her own morning talk show on a local Chicago station. Two years later she gained national recognition for her role in the movie *The Color Purple*. The next year her talk show went national, and before long *The Oprah Winfrey Show* had become the most watched daytime talk show in America.

Richard Wright (1908–1960), a novelist, was born near Natchez. The son of a sharecropper, he first gained fame in 1938 for a collection of short stories called *Uncle Tom's Children*. His writings deal mainly with the struggles of African Americans in a racist society. His best-known novel, *Native Son*, won acclaim for its realism and power. His autobiography, *Black Boy*, captures the pain, fear, pleasures, and hopes that he experienced during his childhood in the South. From 1947 until his death, Wright lived in France because he found less racial prejudice there.

Tammy Wynette (1942–1998), born in Tupelo, was a popular country music star. She taught herself to play piano and guitar and worked in various jobs before heading to Nashville to break into the country-music scene. A regular performer with the Grand Ole Opry beginning in 1969, she had many successful songs, including "Stand By Your Man."

TOUR THE STATE

Beauvoir (Biloxi) This pre–Civil War mansion, the retirement home of Confederate president Jefferson Davis, once served as the Mississippi Confederate Soldiers' Home. The house, filled with Davis family possessions, is open to visitors as a museum. A restored army hospital and a cemetery that includes the Tomb of the Unknown Confederate Soldier are also on the grounds.

Vicksburg National Military Park (Vicksburg) This park preserves trenches, rifle pits, a Confederate cemetery, and other reminders of the siege of Vicksburg during the Civil War.

Natchez Trace Parkway (Natchez to Nashville) The scenic roadway that runs between Natchez and Nashville, Tennessee, follows an ancient trading path established by Native Americans and later used by white settlers. Along the way are picnic sites, nature trails, museums, historic sites, and Indian mounds.

Petrified Forest (Flora) The only petrified forest in the eastern United States, this site contains giant fossilized trees dating from about 36 million years ago. Visitors can wander nature trails, visit a museum devoted to the geology of the region, or browse in the rock and gem shop.

Windsor Castle ruins near Port Gibson

Delta Blues Museum (Clarksdale) This fascinating museum honors the blues music of the South, bringing the music and its performers to life with videos, recordings, photographs, slide shows, and memorabilia.

French Camp Historic Area (French Camp) This restored settlement from the early 1800s features a log cabin and the pre–Civil War home of a Confederate officer. Visitors can view exhibits and watch craft demonstrations and the operation of a grain mill.

Rainwater Observatory (French Camp) This observatory, the largest in Mississippi, provides public access to 20 working telescopes. The observatory also features models of the solar system, astronomy exhibits, and a planetarium that offers daily sky shows.

Florewood River Plantation State Park (Greenwood) The 22 buildings of this full-scale replica of an 1850s cotton plantation provide a close-up look at life in the Old South. The park offers many demonstrations of everyday plantation activities by people in period costumes.

Choctaw Museum of the Southern Indian (Philadelphia) Located on the Choctaw Indian Reservation, this museum contains exhibits on the life and culture of the Choctaw Indians and other southeastern Native American tribes.

Emerald Mound (Natchez) The second-largest Indian ceremonial mound in the nation, Emerald Mound is thought to have been built around 1400. A trail leads to the top of the mound, which offers spectacular views of the surrounding area.

Mount Locust Inn (Natchez) Built around 1780, this is the only remaining example of a frontier inn on the Natchez Trace. Restored to its original appearance, the inn gives visitors a glimpse of the accommodations available to travelers on the frontier in the late 1700s and early 1800s.

NASA John C. Stennis Space Center (Nicholson) NASA uses this center to test systems for the space shuttle and experimental spacecraft. A visitor center provides a look at the U.S. space program and its astronauts.

Dunn's Falls Water Park (Enterprise) This park features a 65-foot waterfall that was once used to power a historic gristmill. It also offers a wildlife refuge, picnic areas, swimming, and hiking trails.

Old Number One Firehouse Museum (Greenville) This firehouse is now a museum that features hands-on displays about firefighting, an area where children can dress up in period costumes, and a big 1927 fire engine named Bertha.

Birthplace of the Frog Exhibit (Leland) Built to commemorate Mississippian Jim Henson, this exhibit displays the original Muppets, including Kermit the Frog. There are also videos of early Henson television shows and Muppet memorabilia.

J. L. Scott Marine Education Center/Aquarium (Biloxi) Located on the campus of the Gulf Coast Research Laboratory, the center features more than 40 large aquariums filled with local sea creatures and plant life.

Hattiesburg Zoo (Hattiesburg) One of the best small zoos in the South features a train ride on a scale-model railroad through acres of animal exhibits. It's both fun and educational.

FUN FACTS

Mississippi is the final resting place of royalty. Rose Hill Cemetery in Meridian contains the graves of Emil and Kelly Mitchell, the king and queen of all the Gypsies in the United States. Since 1915 Gypsies from around the nation have visited the grave to leave small gifts in honor of their royal family.

Although it may never have really rained "cats and dogs," strange things do fall from the sky. On May 11, 1887, during a severe hailstorm near Bovina, a large hailstone fell from the sky. Inside the six-by-eight-inch hailstone was a small gopher turtle completely encased in the ice.

While hunting near Onward, Mississippi, in 1901, President Theodore Roosevelt refused to shoot a small, exhausted bear he came upon in the woods. Soon after, a New Yorker named Morris Michtom designed a stuffed toy bear in honor of the president's action. He called this stuffed bear "Teddy's Bear," which marked the beginning of teddy bears in America.

If people can sing, why not rivers? The Singing River in Pascagoula is famous for the music it makes, which sounds like a swarm of bees. According to legend, the music is the song of two Native Americans who drowned themselves in the river rather than marry others chosen by their families.

FIND OUT MORE

Do you want to know more about Mississippi? Here are some places to start:

BOOKS

General State Books

Aylesworth, Thomas G. and Virginia L. *The South: Alabama, Florida, Mississippi.* New York: Chelsea House, 1995.

Fradin, Dennis B. *Mississippi.* Chicago: Children's Press, 1995.

Thompson, Kathleen. *Mississippi.* Austin, TX: Raintree Steck-Vaughn, 1996.

Special Interest Books

Daniels, Jonathan. *The Devil's Backbone: The Story of the Natchez Trace.* Gretna, LA: Pelican Publishing, 1985.

Herda, D. J. *Historical America: The South Central States.* Brookfield, CT: Millbrook Press, 1993.

McCall, Edith S. *Biography of a River: The Living Mississippi.* New York: Walker & Co., 1990.

Shirley, David. *Every Day I Sing the Blues: The Story of B.B. King.* New York: Franklin Watts, 1995.

Taylor, Mildred D. *Let the Circle Be Unbroken*. New York: Dial Books, 1981.

Twain, Mark. *Life on the Mississippi*. New York: New American Library, 1997.

RECORDINGS

Hooker, John Lee. *The Ultimate Collection*. Rhino.

Howlin' Wolf. *The Chess Box*. Chess MCA.

Johnson, Robert. *King of the Delta Blues*. Columbia.

Presley, Elvis. *The Sun Sessions*. RCA.

Waters, Muddy. *Folk Singer*. Chess MCA.

ONLINE RESOURCES

www.valuecom.com/mississippi—This travel-related service combines up-to-date business and tourist information with a broad range of facts about the state, including summaries of the state's history, economy, geography, natural resources, cultural achievements, and people.

www.state.ms.us—This detailed website presents information about the Mississippi government and related agencies, along with a thorough list of other Mississippi websites.

www.govoff.state.ms.us/misinfo.htm—This official webpage of the Mississippi governor's office presents basic information about the state's government, history, and economics, along with special sections on famous Mississippians and southern recipes.

INDEX

Chart, graph, and illustration page numbers are in boldface.